THE URGENT VOICE

A seldom-viewed picture of William Miller, the man of *The Urgent Voice*, photographed from a painting

THE STORY OF WILLIAM MILLER
THE URGENT VOICE

By
Robert Gale

TEACH Services, Inc.
PUBLISHING
www.TEACHServices.com • (800) 367-1844

World rights reserved. This book or any portion thereof may not be copied or reproduced in any form or manner whatever, except as provided by law, without the written permission of the publisher, except by a reviewer who may quote brief passages in a review.

The author assumes full responsibility for the accuracy of all facts and quotations as cited in this book. The opinions expressed in this book are the author's personal views and interpretations, and do not necessarily reflect those of the publisher.

This book is provided with the understanding that the publisher is not engaged in giving spiritual, legal, medical, or other professional advice. If authoritative advice is needed, the reader should seek the counsel of a competent professional.

Copyright © 2006, 2019 Robert Gale
Copyright © 2019 TEACH Services, Inc.
ISBN-13: 978-1-57258-447-1 (Paperback)
Library of Congress Control Number: 2006905028

CONTENTS

1782–1810	Boy to Man	1
1810–1815	Deist and Soldier	9
1815–1818	From Doubt to Faith	21
1818–1831	Miller and the Monomaniac	29
1831–1833	Miller: A Household Word	33
1833–1840	A New Era	43
1840–1843	Methods and Means	63
1843	Headache and Heartache	77
1843–1844	Come Out of Her, My People	89
	Unto 2300 Days	99
1844	March 21–October 22, Days of Glory	107
1844	New Light	117
1844–1845	Time of Gloom	127
1845–1849	The Silenced Voice	141
Appendix:	Important Dates and Events in William Miller's Life	147

CHAPTER 1
1782–1810
BOY TO MAN

William threw back the quilts and crawled quietly out of his warm bed. Then, cautiously opening the bedroom door, he slipped into the large main room, which was lighted by the moonlight streaming through the window and by embers that glowed in the fireplace. Going to the fireplace, he found in the firewood piled nearby a large pine knot he had placed there that afternoon. He held it for a few moments against the live embers. The knot burst into flame, and he positioned it carefully so that it cast its light upon the floor. This done, he stretched out full length upon his stomach on the floor, with a book open before him. Twelve-year-old William Miller was enjoying his favorite pastime.

It was the year 1794, and life was hard for the Miller family. Long hours each day of manual labor and years of privation and continuous hardship were their common lot, as they were for most pioneer families of early America. It took all the energy that available hands could supply to fell the trees, clear the ground, construct the necessary rough log buildings, plant the crops, and reap the meager harvest on the 100-acre farm in the semi-wilderness of New York. And the twenty bushels of wheat that were required as annual payment on the lease were never easy to come by. Even the help of 12-year-old William was essential if ends were to be met. "Early to bed" was the rule, for everyone must be up and about by sunrise. Daylight was a precious commodity in those times.

In common with other pioneer families, the Millers were forced to practice the most rigid economy. Candles were a luxury they could ill afford; but William had learned, as had many other boys under similar circumstances, that a good pine knot gives off more light than several candles. And knots were free for the gathering.

William was a favorite name in the Miller family. Grandfather William Miller had settled in Pittsfield, Massachusetts, about 1747, soon after he had married Hannah Leonard. To them had been born three sons and a daughter. One of the sons died in infancy. The other two, Elihu and William, married and produced large families as was common in that day, a custom born of economic necessity. This William also named one of his sons William. This son, the oldest of sixteen children—five sons and eleven daughters—is the subject of this biography.

Father William Miller was a captain in the Colonial army and served during the Revolutionary War. On March 22, 1781, soon after returning to civilian life, he married Paulina Phelps, daughter of a Baptist minister. The newly married couple settled near the bride's home in Pittsfield. Their son, William, was born there on February 15, 1782, four months after Cornwallis' surrender at Yorktown. In 1786, when William was 4 years old, the family moved to a farm at Low Hampton, New York, close to the Vermont line. There, on what was then the Western frontier, William Miller grew to manhood.

Educational opportunities in the newly settled area around Low Hampton were extremely limited. During most of William's boyhood, school—when it existed at all—was held only during the winter months, when the boys' help could best be spared from the farm. But the long winter evenings helped to make up for the short school terms; for it was during these evenings that William's mother taught him to read, using the few books the family owned—the Bible, the psalter, and the prayer book.

Early in life William developed a love of reading and a thirst for knowledge that increased as he grew older. The time came when he begged his father for a copy of *The History of Crusoe*. His father finally consented to buy the book—on condition that William earn the money by chopping wood during his spare time. As if there were any spare time. But somehow he earned the money and bought his book. As soon as he could he bought another book, *The Adventures of Robert Boyle.*

People of the community who became interested in William and his passion for reading began to lend him books. When this voluntary supply became exhausted he sought out families whom he suspected might have books he could borrow. In this way he satisfied to some extent his increasing desire for knowledge. So, like another boy, named Abraham Lincoln, who was born on the frontier a quarter of a century later, William received an important part of his education on the floor in front of the fireplace.

On the occasion described at the beginning of our story, William's reading was interrupted by the sound of footsteps. He had time only to look up from his book before his father appeared in the doorway. Father Miller, upon a chance awakening, had seen the flickering light and dancing shadows that William's pine knot cast upon the wall. Fearing that the house was on fire—a misfortune all too common in those days of open fireplaces—he had lost no time in investigating. When he saw William sprawled on the floor, his relief gave way to sudden anger. Grabbing a whip that lay coiled upon the hearth, he cried, "Bill, if you don't go to bed, I'll horsewhip you!"

William probably discontinued his late night reading, at least for a while. But he was always careful to see that there was a pine knot ready to be used when he wanted it. One day one of his sisters mistakenly used his knot as kindling to start a stubborn fire. When he discovered the loss he became so upset he impulsively slapped her. This was the only time he was known to abuse her in any way.

Young William inherited a strong body, which was strengthened by farm work; and he had a well-developed mind for his age, which he kept alert by reading at every opportunity. The result was that after he had attended the local school with its meager facilities for only a few years, it became apparent he had nothing to gain by continued attendance there. He furthered his education by reading and studying by the light of the fireplace.

While in his early teens William began to keep a diary. Thus early in life he began to show an interest in writing, as well as in reading. The date on the title page is "July 10th, 1797," when he was 15. In boyish style, he headed the diary "The History of My Life." On the first page he wrote, "I was early educated and taught to pray the Lord." In this entry we catch a glimpse of the spiritual influence of his home on his early years. But this was not unusual in pioneer America where in many homes daily reading of the Bible and family prayers were part of the normal routine. In most respects, William grew up like other young boys of his day on the Western frontier.

In time the financial circumstances of the Miller family improved. The log house was replaced by a comfortable frame building, which had a room for William. Now he could buy a new book occasionally. And candles took the place of the pine knots, which permitted him to study in the comfort of his room.

As he grew older and his mental horizons widened, William became conscious that he possessed ambitions that he could never realize with the limited financial resources his father's meager income provided. A local physician, a Dr. Smith, was relatively wealthy for his time; and, like many in his profession, he had a reputation for being liberal in the interest of worthy causes. After considerable mental anguish, and without consulting his parents, William one day sat down and wrote a letter to the good doctor. He expressed the inner longings of his young heart, told of his desire for an education, explained the family financial situation, and asked the doctor for help. He had hardly completed the letter when his father entered the room. This presented an awkward situation that resulted in his father's reading the letter.

The letter deeply affected William's father. For the first time in his life he felt dissatisfied, not because of any shortcomings on his part, but because of his son's desires and ambitions, previously considered an annoyance, which he now saw in a new light. He was realistic enough to know that William's aspirations, so poignantly expressed in the letter, could never be fulfilled. But the knowledge that his son harbored such aspirations touched and melted the father's heart. William's letter was never mailed. But in that room that day father and son shed tears together, and spoke words of mutual sympathy and understanding. From that time, the father was less severe with William, and William was more sympathetic with his father.

In his later teens William's gift with the pen and his ability to handle words became increasingly apparent. He became what his friend and biographer, Sylvester Bliss, called the "scribbler general" among the younger set. If one wanted a verse composed or a letter written with special flair, William Miller was the one to call upon.

After the Revolutionary War ended, the territory along the Northern frontier of the New England States and New York was opened for settlement. Many families from Massachusetts, Rhode Island, and Connecticut migrated to the new frontier. Among the families that moved from New York were the Millers, who left Low Hampton to establish a new home near the community of Poultney, Vermont.

Another family new to the area were the Smiths, who settled about twelve miles from the Millers. Twelve miles was a considerable distance in those days. But the Smiths had relatives who lived in the immediate neighborhood of the Millers, so it was not strange that William met Lucy Smith, a girl about his own age. Acquaintance developed into friendship, and friendship soon blossomed into love.

In his diary under the date of January 2, 1803, William made this entry: "Be it remembered that on this day, it being a Sunday in the afternoon of the aforesaid day, I did bind myself and was bound to be, the partner of Miss Lucy Smith, of Poultney, and by these presents do agree to be hers and only hers till death shall part us (provided she is of the same mind). Whereunto I here set my hand and seal."

This is not very romantic language for a young man to use in writing about his engagement. Indeed, it is so formal as to suggest that William may have included some books on law in his reading. But it also suggests that he realized the seriousness of the pact into which he had entered.

Evidently, Lucy was "of the same mind," for they were married on June 29, 1803, when William was 21 years of age. Shortly after their marriage they established a new home in Poultney, near the home of Lucy's parents. To William and Lucy Miller were eventually born ten children, seven sons and three daughters. Two of the children, however, did not live beyond infancy.

Soon after he was married, William became a member of the Masonic fraternity, in which he eventually advanced to the highest order. Before his marriage he joined the militia and rose to the rank of sergeant. This was his first position in anything that resembled a public office. But in 1809, six years after his marriage, he became a deputy sheriff. His first entry in the record of writs served bears the date of December 6, 1809. In the years to follow he was at different times a deputy sheriff, constable, and justice of the peace.

In those days, soon after America had severed its political ties with England, the nation and its communities entered into the spirit of celebrating Independence Day with more enthusiasm than is common today. Inspired by the feeling of patriotism that permeated the air during the preparation for one particular Independence Day, William composed a poem while hoeing in his cornfield. He adapted the meter to the rhythm of a popular song of the day. But, after having written the poem, he was too timid to tell anyone about it. Then one day he "accidentally" dropped a copy of the poem under a window of the home of a certain Mr. Ashley. By "coincidence" Mr. Ashley was the man who had charge of the community's celebration. Mr. Ashley's wife found the poem a few minutes later. Assuming it had been blown out of her husband's study, she placed the copy on his desk. As William had hoped, Mr. Ashley decided the poem was just what he needed to put the finishing touch to the day's celebration. Although he did not know the author, he had it printed and distributed at the proper time.

One of those who helped to distribute the poem was an Elder Kendrick, a Baptist minister who was an acquaintance of Miller's, though not a close friend. But Kendrick had his own idea as to the authorship of the poem, and Miller's facial expressions and actions when he received his copy confirmed Kendrick's suspicion. When he was questioned, Miller had no choice but to tell the truth. The word soon spread. The public singing of the hymn made a deep impression upon the community. It brought William to the favorable attention of the people of Poultney, and he became somewhat of a local celebrity. The following stanzas of the poem give some idea as to the thought and style:

> *Our independence dear,*
> *Bought with the price of blood,*
> *Let us receive with care,*
> *And trust our Maker, God,*
> *For He's the tower*
> *To which we fly;*
> *His grace is nigh*
> *In every hour!*

> *Let traitors hide their heads,*
> *And party quarrels cease;*
> *Our foes are struck with dread.*
> *When we declare for peace,*
> *Firm let us be,*
> *And rally round*
> *The glorious sound*
> *Of liberty!*

CHAPTER 2
1810–1815
DEIST AND SOLDIER

A few months after the Independence celebration, Miller made a decision that probably puzzled his friends, and perhaps surprised his family, as well. In what seems to have been a rather abrupt move, he exchanged the life of a farmer for that of a soldier. We may never know all the reasons for this change. It seems obvious he was motivated to some degree by the same feeling of patriotism that inspired him to write his poem. The military service of his father may also have influenced his decision.

There was at least one other factor. He had become disillusioned with humanity, and hoped that in the service of his country he might find a satisfaction, a certain something, that thus far had escaped him. This disappointment with his fellow beings was more the result of his reading than of personal experience.

It seemed to Miller that the more he read of history, the more dreadful man's character appeared. The conquerors of the world, the supposed heroes of history, were in reality only demons in human form. All the world's misery seemed to be increased in direct proportion to the power these would-be heroes exerted over their fellow men. It was in this state of mind that Miller entered military service, with the hope that in the love of country he might find at least one bright spot in human character.

What kind of person was William Miller, this man whose name in a few years was to become synonymous with religious fanaticism and who, with his teachings, was to become the object of public ridicule to a degree experienced by few people?

He enjoyed the confidence of his fellow citizens of Poultney. This is shown by the fact that when he was required to furnish bond on assuming the office of deputy sheriff, the response was such that several times the required amount was made available by friends and neighbors in the community.

He was not intemperate in his habits or profane in his speech. In brief, he was what we commonly consider a "good man," with no apparent offensive habits. He was outwardly a moral man, but at this period in his life he made no pretense of being a Christian.

As a boy—"between the ages of seven and ten," in his own words—he had suffered from a deep sense of guilt, and spent much time and effort trying to win God's approval and feel free from sin. As is often the case with children, and not infrequently with adults, he first tried to secure relief from his guilt feelings by resolving to be "very good." "I will do nothing wrong, tell no lies, and obey my parents," he determined. But, like others who try that, he learned that good resolutions by themselves, without the indwelling power of the Holy Spirit, do not bring peace with God or victory in one's life. Looking for another solution, he decided to try sacrifice. "I will give up the most cherished objects I possess," he promised. But this also failed to bring satisfaction. His inward conflicts continued for some years. In 1803, the year of his marriage, when he was 21, he expressed his wish in these poetic lines:

> Come, blest Religion, with thy angel's face,
> Dispel this gloom, and brighten all the place;
> Drive this destructive passion from my breast;
> Compose my sorrows, and restore my rest;
> Show me the path that Christian heroes trod,
> Wean me from earth, and raise my soul to God![1]

But Miller's prayer for spiritual peace was not to be answered for some years. Perhaps the experience he longed for was delayed by the influence of his friends.

The young men with whom he associated at Poultney were not immoral. Like Miller, they were "good men," good citizens, honest, humane, and generous. But their thinking was permeated by skeptical principles and deistic theories. They rejected the Bible as the revelation of truth and the

---

1   *A Brief History of William Miller, the Great Pioneer in Adventist Faith* (Washington, D.C.: Review and Herald, 1915), 34.

standard of life. They bolstered their beliefs with the writings of Voltaire, Hume, Paine, and others of the same type. In his wide reading, Miller too had delved into tainted religious philosophy. So, under the influence of atheistic writings and the pressure of his friends, he joined them in their belief. He announced that he too was a deist. F. D. Nichol aptly calls deism "that halfway station on the road to atheism." Deism does not disbelieve in God, but views Him as an impersonal, absentee landlord, uninterested in man's personal affairs.

In writing later about this period of his life, Miller stated, "Thus, from 1804 to 1816, I was a firm, and, as I then thought, a consistent, opposer of the Christian faith." The deistical influence of his reading and friends made subtle but serious inroads upon the spiritual experience of the man who as a boy had been "taught to pray the Lord."

But there is reason to believe that even during those twelve years he retained some degree of confidence in the Bible; that he was even then searching for something more assuring than his deistical beliefs afforded him. Certain sentiments expressed in his letters indicate that he was not at heart the dyed-in-the-wool deist he professed to be.

However, it was during this time, while he was under the influence of his nonbelieving friends and while he himself was a professing deist, that his life sank to its lowest level. It was as though, having announced his deistical beliefs openly, he felt the need of proving his profession. This he did on frequent occasions by mimicking the devotional services of his family for the entertainment of his friends.

There were two relatives whose spiritual experience, especially, became the butt of his "jokes" and the object of his ridicule. Perhaps this was because, of all the family, their devotion was to him the greatest rebuke, a constant reminder of the experience he had once coveted. One of these relatives was his Grandfather Phelps, pastor of the Baptist church at Orwell. The other was his uncle, Elihu Miller, pastor of the Baptist church at Low Hampton. Both were men of strong character and ardent devotion, though they were somewhat lacking in the social graces. This was a combination that Miller found especially suitable for his purpose. Both men were frequent guests in the Miller home at Poultney, and although William received them graciously and entertained them generously, he made them the objects of his "humor," mimicking their words, voices, and gestures with great exaggeration, much to the amusement of his friends.

William was mistaken if he thought his sacrilegious actions were unknown to his family. The person most affected was his mother, who shed many tears over the matter. Upon those few occasions when she shared her burden with her father, Pastor Phelps, who knew that he also was the object of William's pantomime, his response invariably was, "Don't worry about William. There is something yet for him to do in the cause of God!" William may not have known that those at whose expense he was entertaining his friends were even then praying for his conversion. And he could not know that in answer to their prayers he would indeed have a work to do in the cause of God. He could not know that what he was measuring out to them in ridicule would in the future be measured out to him, pressed down, shaken together, and running over. This was the William Miller who entered the service of his country with the hope of finding "one bright spot."

In those days, any man who could persuade a company of men to join the army and make him their captain, could enter the army with a captaincy. The fact that Miller succeeded in bringing forty-seven men with him into military service speaks well for his standing in the community and testifies to his leadership ability.

In the life of a soldier, saying goodby to friends and family is an experience that brings mixed emotions. Feelings of sorrow and gladness, bravery and timidity, usually are intermingled. There was a public farewell when the men of Miller's company took official leave of their families, community, and civil life, to take up arms in service to their country. Miller's friends expected that as a deist he would use his influence to see that this occasion was nothing more than a mere ceremony. They were surprised therefore when he concluded his company's farewell by asking Elder Kendrick to offer a prayer.

Miller's company was ordered to Burlington, Vermont. Soon after he arrived there with his men he was transferred from the Vermont State Volunteers to the regular United States Army, with the rank of lieutenant. He was almost immediately ordered to report back to Rutland County, his home territory, as a recruiting officer. Not until the Civil War did the United States operate a selective service or draft system; consequently, in Miller's time the country depended entirely upon volunteers for all branches of the service, which made the work of the recruiting officers of prime importance. Even at that date, two years before the outbreak of the War of 1812, a feeling of impending conflict was in the air. The political and military situation was such that the Government badly needed men who could be relied upon to protect the country from an expected invasion from Canada. Miller was generally known and highly respected in the area to which he was assigned, and the success with which he carried out his duties demonstrated the wisdom of his superiors in assigning him to that particular vicinity. And no doubt the assignment was very acceptable to Miller, for it permitted him to stay in his own home.

On June 1, 1812, President Madison asked Congress to declare war against Great Britain. Lieutenant Miller continued his duties as a recruiting officer until 1814, but the convenience of staying in his own home came to an abrupt end in July, 1813, when he received orders to join his regiment at Burlington.

Several months later, after taking part in a few skirmishes that closed the campaign of 1813, Miller received another order dated January 10, 1814, reassigning him to recruiting duties throughout the State of Vermont.

The year 1814 was crucial in the war between the United States and Great Britain. In the early part of that year, while still serving as a recruiting officer, Miller was promoted to the rank of captain in the U.S. Army. With the promotion came larger responsibilities that placed him in a different relationship to his men. Under the previous command, discipline had become lax, and morale was low. The anticipated military crisis made it imperative that every

14 • THE URGENT VOICE

company and every soldier be at peak efficiency. This situation forced upon the new captain some unpleasant duties.

Some of the problems Miller faced, and the solutions he proposed, are alluded to in this letter written to his wife:

>Camp near Fort Moreau, in Plattsburgh,
>September 4th, 1814, Sunday, 9 o'clock evening
>
>DEAR LucY: I received your letter of the 30th, and perceived by the contents, that you received only eighty dollars. I enclosed one hundred, and think you must have been mistaken; for, if any person had robbed the letter, they would have taken the whole. My soldiers were paid their money today, and I have had to go out twice, since I have begun this letter, to still the noise. I have found the company in a very wayward situation, but believe by dint of application, I shall be able to bring them to good subordination. I have had to punish four or five of them very severely, and have reason to believe that they both love and fear me. One look is now sufficient to quell any disorder. This we call a payday, and, once in four days, we have a whiskey-day; on which days, I have six or seven soldiers who will take a little too much, and then, of all the devils in hell, I think they must exceed in deviltry.
>
>But this is only the bad picture. In my next letter, I will show you the good side. The British are within ten miles of this place, and we expect a battle tomorrow;...it may be my lot to fall; if I do, I will fall bravely. Remember, you will never hear from me, if I am a coward. I must close, as it is almost 11 o'clock. Remember your
>
>WM. MILLER[2]

The engagement that Miller had momentarily expected did not take place until almost a week later. It became known as the Battle of Plattsburgh, named after the scene of the action, which was on the western shore of Lake Champlain, about twenty miles south of the Canadian border and approximately one hundred miles from the Miller home in Poultney.

The Battle of Plattsburgh was fought on Sunday, September 11, 1814. That morning Lucy Miller was unusually concerned for her husband's safety. She seems to have had

2   Ibid., 36, 37.

a premonition he would not survive the anticipated battle he had mentioned in his previous letter. Nothing her family or friends did—not reasoning, argument, or ridicule—could calm her fears. It appears that not until evening did the emotional strain leave her. Even then she continued to have a great fear for her husband's life.

Near the close of the next day a messenger on horseback brought the good news of victory, which was quickly relayed to the entire area by the village bell. Such news may satisfy the patriot and historian; it may not console the wife or mother, for victory is often purchased at the highest possible price. No doubt many had died in battle. Was William among them? Lucy Miller had no way of knowing until the arrival of the next mail from the scene of war. Her premonition proved to be wrong, for the mail soon brought a letter written on Monday, which assured her of his having survived the battle.

The Americans, with 1,500 regulars and about 4,000 volunteers, had defeated the British who were 15,000 strong. With the odds so much in favor of the British, the Americans thought their own defeat was almost certain. The unexpected victory made an indelible impression upon Miller's thinking. He could account for the victory only in the light of Providence, and this disturbed his deistical thinking.

Although the Battle of Plattsburgh put an end to the hostilities in that area, the troops continued to be stationed there as a precautionary measure. The letters Miller wrote during this period gives us a clue to his thinking.

The last of October he wrote Lucy a letter in which he related the death of one of his men, Spencer, who had been an acquaintance of the Millers as a civilian. The concluding paragraph shows his ideas concerning a future life.

> But a short time, and, like Spencer, I shall be no more. It is a solemn thought. Yet, could I be sure of one other life, there would be nothing terrific; but to go out like an extinguished taper [candle], is insupportable—the thought is doleful. No; rather let me cling to that hope which warrants a neverending existence;...where neverending spring shall flourish, and love, pure as the driven snow, rest in every breast.

It seems evident that if Miller ever really believed in the deistic doctrine of annihilation, it became increasingly unacceptable to him as time passed, and that it contributed to his eventual rejection of deism.

Miller's weaning from deism was gradual. In 1812 he had expressed serious doubts regarding his being able to accept the teaching of deism completely. But he still could not bring himself to accept the Bible as inspired.

On November 11, 1814, he wrote a letter to his wife that sheds light on his thinking. He first referred to a promise Lucy had made to write to him "every Monday morning." Then he chided her for neglecting to write the previous Monday by addressing the remaining paragraphs of the letter to their children on the assumption that "my Lucy is no more."

In these paragraphs Miller gave some advice one would hardly expect from a genuine deist. He admonished the children that their "first study" ought to lead them to look up to the Supreme Being as the Author of all things; and that they should ever keep in mind that "he sees every action of your life, knows every thought, and hears every word." Miller expressed the hope that his son William would "set so good an example to your brothers and sisters, as that, if they should follow it, shall insure them peace, love, and friendship here, and happiness in the world to come."

It would seem from the expression of such sentiments that some cracks, if not actual breaks, were appearing in the wall that Miller the deist had built up against Christianity.

If Miller entered the army with the hope of discovering the better side of human nature, he no doubt was disappointed, for the armed services have never been known as schools of morality. It was Miller's observation of such practices as intemperance, immorality, gambling, and stealing that eventually sickened him of army life.

However, there are always some staunch characters who are not contaminated by exposure to such society. And there were in Miller's Thirtieth Infantry Regiment a few men of piety, prayer, and religious conviction in spite of their unchristian surroundings. Such a man was Sergeant Willey, whose tent was frequently used by some of the men as a place of prayer.

On one occasion Miller, the officer of the day, saw a light in the sergeant's tent at an unusually late hour. Wanting to know what was going on—which was in line with his duty— he approached the tent. One of the men was praying. He did not disturb the group, but determined to test Willey's piety and at the same time play a joke on him.

The next morning he had Willey called before him. Pretending great seriousness, with a voice bordering on severity, he said, "You know, Sergeant Willey, that it is contrary to the army regulations to have any gambling in the tents at night. And I was very sorry to see your tent lit up, for that purpose, last night. We cannot have any gambling at such times. You must put a stop to it at once."

Poor Willey was shocked to hear such an accusation brought against himself and his comrades. Embarrassed, hardly daring to look up, he stated simply, "We were not gambling, sir."

But pressing Willey further in a voice even more stern than before, Miller replied, "Yes, you were gambling. And it won't do." And then testing the bewildered soldier again, he asked,

"What else could you have your tent lighted up for, all the evening, if you were not gambling?"

Recognizing the necessity of being more explicit in his explanation, the sergeant answered, "We were praying, sir."

At heart Miller was really a tender man, and by this time he was almost in tears. But he was determined to go through with his little act. With a motion of the hand he indicated that the young soldier was to leave. He could not risk being betrayed by his voice. For some time after Willey's withdrawal, Miller remained alone, pondering the courage of these Christian men in their unchristian surroundings, and meditating upon the somewhat questionable course of action his little joke had caused him to take.

Although it appears that Miller succeeded to a large degree in insulating himself from the low morality practiced by many of his men, he did not remain entirely uncontaminated by the evil practices to which he was constantly exposed. There were two undesirable habits that he took with him to civilian life. However, he dropped them in a short time.

He later wrote about one of these habits, "One day in May, 1816, I detected myself in the act of taking the name of God in vain—a habit I acquired in the service; and I was instantly convicted of its sinfulness."

The second habit was gambling. This, too, he abandoned soon after returning home at the close of the war. Evidence indicates that Miller's high regard for the principles of personal virtue, and especially his avoidance of even the slightest violation of the laws of chastity, made him at times the sport of his less scrupulous fellow officers.

Although the war came to a close officially with the signing of the Treaty of Ghent on December 24, 1814, the army that fought at Plattsburgh remained there until after the official ratification on February 6, 1815. Soon after that, Miller, with five years of military service behind him, returned to civilian life. He had entered the service with the hope of finding a satisfaction he had failed to find elsewhere. "But," he wrote later, "two years in the service was enough to convince me that I was in error in this thing also. When I left the service, I had become completely disgusted with man's public character."

Miller's personal integrity and official honor throughout his military career were such as to command the respect and affection of those who served under him. For some time after the close of the war it was rather common for his fellow officers, as well as the men who had served under him, to stop at his home for a visit. Some of them, whom fortune did not treat kindly after the war, made the Miller home their headquarters for days, or even weeks.

One incident will illustrate the high esteem placed upon Miller's judgment by two of his fellow soldiers. Soon after the close of the war these former members of Miller's company found themselves living as neighbors in northern Vermont. In time they had a disagreement over a business deal, which eventually became so serious that they could hardly tolerate each other. They both often thought of their former captain, whose judgment they had learned to respect, and wished that their difficulty could be submitted to him for settlement. But the distance involved and the resulting expense in time and money seemed to make this impossible. Yet the misunderstanding grew more serious with each passing week and began to involve others in the neighborhood. At last, in spite of obstacles, they decided to visit Mr. Miller and submit their case to him. They agreed that each was to tell his side of the story and then willingly abide by Miller's decision. The two men made the trip separately, but arrived at Miller's home about the same time. After each had presented his case, Miller made a decision that the men accepted. They shook hands, visited with their former captain briefly, and returned together to their respective homes as friends and neighbors.

Chapter 3
1815–1818
FROM DOUBT TO FAITH

When Miller's military career ended, a new era of his life began, the results of which he could never have foreseen. In that year he moved his family from Poultney, Vermont, to Low Hampton, New York. His father had died at Low Hampton in 1812, leaving the homestead with a heavy mortgage, which Miller paid off. When he left the army his mother and brother, Solomon, were living on the old farm. Miller bought another farm half a mile to the west, where he resumed civilian life, having no other expectation than to remain a farmer the rest of his days.

On this property Miller erected a new farmhouse in 1815. Of wood-frame construction, two stories high, it differed very little from dozens of other farm homes built during that period. It was neat and "good-looking," but was not the largest or the handsomest in the community.

West of the house a few rods was a beautiful grove, which was selected as the site of the community's celebration of independence on July 4, 1816. To Miller went the honor of being the marshal of the occasion, and he used his influence in that capacity to see that all persons in the area were invited to participate in the festivities, regardless of party affiliation. In that era of extreme party loyalty and political excitement, this was considered to be a wonderfully charitable gesture.

In the earlier days of Low Hampton there had been no church in the community, so Miller's Grandfather Phelps had made a practice of holding services in the home of Miller's father whenever he made his occasional visits to the farm. As a result of these services, Miller's mother had been converted and a "company" had been organized as a branch of the Baptist church of Orwell, Vermont. By 1812 a small meetinghouse had been erected. The pastor was Elisha Miller, William's uncle.

After William left the army and moved to Low Hampton, he began to attend the little church there, although he was not a professing Christian. Perhaps his attendance was encouraged by his relationship to the pastor. More likely, he went out of respect to his mother's wishes. Or it may be that he was at heart more in sympathy with Christian ideals and practices than he cared to admit. Whatever his feelings or motives were, his attendance at the church became quite regular.

There were times, however, when the pastor was absent because of duties at other churches in his district. In his absence the church service was conducted by a leading layman who read a sermon instead of attempting to preach. The sermon was usually selected from *Proudfoot's Practical Sermons*.

Miller's mother soon noticed that her son's occasional absences from church coincided with the pastor's absences. When she remonstrated with him about this, he replied that he did not find the readings edifying, and implied that if *he* could do the reading, he would attend. If this sounds like boasting, we must remember that those who did the reading may not have been especially skilled in the art. Miller, on the other hand, had always been an avid reader, with a certain native skill in the use of words. It is, of course, possible that he was being somewhat facetious when he made the statement. But regardless of what his reason may have been, his mother recognized an opportunity when she saw one. She evidently conveyed the information to the right persons, for after that, Miller was asked to read the sermon in the pastor's absence. The deacons, however, continued to choose the selection that was to be read.

From several incidents that took place during this time in Miller's life, it is evident that the Holy Spirit was working on his heart. The soldier who had retired from military life was fighting a different kind of battle. It was about this time that he realized he had a habit—picked up in the army, he said—of taking God's name in vain. Convicted of its sinfulness he went to a secluded spot in the grove near his home where he spent time in meditating on the works of nature and the manifestations of Providence. He may have hesitated to call it prayer, but he soon gained the victory over his habit of profanity.

Questions about a future life plagued Miller's thinking. He had time for some leisure reading, and the more he read, the less comfort he found in his deistical views. In his words, "The heavens were as brass over my head, and the earth as iron under my feet. *Eternity—what was it? And death—why was it?* The more I reasoned, the further I was from demonstration. The more I thought, the more scattered were my conclusions. I tried to stop thinking, but my thoughts would not be controlled. I was truly wretched, but did not understand *the cause.* I mourned, but without hope." He continued in this agitated state of mind for many months.

In the meantime, the people of Low Hampton were making plans to celebrate the second anniversary of the Battle of Plattsburgh, September 11, 1816. Enthusiasm was running high. As a participant in the battle, Miller entered into the spirit of the occasion with all the ardor at his command.

Part of the celebration was to be a ball in the neighboring town of Fairhaven. While preparations were being made for the ball, it was announced that a certain minister would speak on the evening prior to the ball. Mostly out of curiosity, Miller and a group of his friends decided to attend the preaching service. They left Miller's home in high spirits.

But when they returned home later that evening, their attitude and behavior had completely changed. Their high glee was gone, they were seriously meditative and had lost their appetite for the ball to be held the next evening. Feelings of deep spiritual humility so permeated the group that the festivities were indefinitely postponed. The solemnity spread from family to family, and meetings of prayer and praise took the place of mirth and merriment in many homes of the community.

On the next Sunday it was Miller's lot to read the sermon in the pastor's absence. The reading that had been chosen for that day was on "The Importance of Parental Duties," usually considered a very uninteresting subject. But as Miller read, the Holy Spirit used something in the article to appeal to his heart. So overpowering was the experience that he was unable to continue reading and had to sit down before he had finished. More than any other, this event marked his conversion, the beginning of a new life.

From that time Miller accepted the Scriptures as a revelation from God. Studying them became his chief delight, and he marveled that he could have rejected them as he had.

Following his conversion, Miller publicly confessed his new faith by becoming a member of the church he had formerly ridiculed. He began the practice of family worship and opened his home for prayer meetings. Entering into his new church relationship with characteristic enthusiasm, he soon became a very active member.

Miller's deist friends were disappointed and dismayed at his new profession of faith, for they had regarded him as a standard-bearer and spokesman for their cause, which he indeed had been. But now they had to regard him as an opponent, an antagonist who knew the weaknesses, as well as the strengths, of their position. For Miller knew from experience exactly what weapons to use, and the points at which those weapons could be aimed most successfully. His former friends took the initiative by assailing the very point he had previously attacked in his assault upon Christianity. In the past, Miller had ridiculed his Christian friends for having "blind faith" in the Bible, which contained ideas that admittedly they could not fully explain. He had found a certain satisfaction in intentionally putting to them perplexing questions and in watching them squirm as they attempted an answer. Or he had rejoiced in triumph when they were forced to admit they had no answer.

But now the tables were turned. Soon after his conversion Miller was talking with a deist friend about the prospects of eternal life through the merits and intercession of Christ. When the friend asked how he knew there was such a Saviour, Miller replied that He was revealed in the Bible. And then the question Miller had tauntingly asked others was addressed to him: *"But how do you know the Bible is true?"* And the question was followed by a reiteration of Miller's former arguments on the apparent contradictions and mysticism that seemed to shroud the problem.

Miller felt the sting of such taunts deeply and at first was at a loss as to how to answer. But he soon concluded that if the Bible is true, as he now believed it to be, it must be consistent with itself; all of its parts must harmonize. Furthermore, he reasoned, it had been given to man for his instruction; therefore, it was adapted to man's understanding. So Miller's reply to such questions became, "Give me time, and I will harmonize all those apparent contradictions to my own satisfaction, or I will be a deist still."

With this determination, he embarked upon a prayerful and detailed study of the Bible. In order not to be influenced by the thinking or interpretation of others, he discarded the use of all commentaries. He quickly saw that he must be careful to distinguish between what the Bible actually says and what it is *thought* to say as interpreted by various groups and individuals. Believing that the Bible must be its own interpreter, he used *Cruden's Concordance* and marginal references as his only helps.

He began with Genesis, and read verse by verse, going only as fast as he could progress with understanding. Whenever he came to a difficult passage he would compare it with all related texts, using the concordance as his help. Only when he had arrived at an explanation that to him was completely satisfactory in light of all other texts, would he go on to the next verse. In this way, comparing scripture with scripture, he studied the entire Bible, taking about two years to complete the project. Before he finished he was fully satisfied that the Bible is its own best expositor.

Some years later, after Miller had become a public figure with a reputation as a student of Bible prophecy, a clergyman once called to see him. Upon being informed that Miller was not at home, the visitor asked for the privilege of seeing his library. So Miller's daughter conducted him into the northeast room that served as Miller's study.

"That is his library," the daughter said, pointing to the two books upon the table—Miller's old family Bible and his concordance. The minister was of course surprised, for he had supposed that so deep a student as Miller would have a library of many volumes. But so far as his theological books were concerned, the daughter's statement was true. Miller never had a commentary in his home, and could not remember having read any book on Bible prophecy except a little in Newton and Faber when he first became a Christian. His old family Bible had cost $18.50; and his copy of *Cruden's Concordance*, purchased in 1798, had cost $8.00. He read almost nothing but these two books.

Miller developed a high regard for the Bible as the Word of God. He considered it a great storehouse of truth from which the student must bring together all the texts on the subject he wished to study, letting every word have its own scriptural meaning and every sentence its proper bearing on the subject.

Miller noticed in his study that many prophetic events in the Bible had been literally fulfilled within specified time limits. As predicted, the Flood came after Noah preached 120 years; Israel sojourned in Egypt 430 years and left on schedule, "the self-same day" (Ex. 12:51); the famine in the time of Joseph lasted seven years as foretold. The Bible contains many examples of time prophecy's being fulfilled on schedule.

It would be impossible for an intelligent, thinking person to study the Bible as thoroughly as Miller did over a period of years, without arriving at some definite conclusions. His conclusions influenced his thinking and his actions for the rest of his life. They resulted in the movement that came to be known as Millerism. This movement became a prominent part of the religious scene of America and to a smaller degree of other countries during the 1830's and 1840's. In fact, the impact of the movement is felt in the religious community even today to a greater extent than many people realize.

What unique conclusions did Miller arrive at? How did his beliefs differ from the teaching of other Bible scholars? We shall let him answer for himself:

While thus studying the Scriptures, I became satisfied... that the popular views of the spiritual reign of Christ—a temporal millennium before the end of the world, and the Jews' return—are not sustained by the word of God....I was then satisfied, as I saw conclusive evidence to prove the advent personal and pre-millennial...and that...the advent of the Lord, instead of being looked for only in the distant future, might be a continually-expected event.

"The advent *personal* and *pre-millennial*"—these were the points on which Miller differed with most of his contemporaries; these were the points that gave his message its uniqueness; these were the points of his teaching that were later to inspire ridicule and abuse.

It was not Miller's purpose to discover "new truth," to begin a new religious movement, or to bring disunity among the churches. He began his study of the Bible with no other purpose than to learn its true teaching. He began his study "with no expectation of finding the time of the Savior's coming, and I could at first hardly believe the result to which I had arrived; but the evidence struck me with such force that I could not resist my convictions. I became nearly settled in my conclusions, and began to wait, and watch, and pray for my Savior's coming."

After a thorough study of the Bible, during a period of two years, from 1816 to 1818, Miller was forced to arrive at two conclusions: The second advent of Christ was "personal and pre-millennial," and the Advent would occur "in about twenty-five years"; that is "about A.D. 1843." In another chapter we shall examine briefly the Bible prophecy that served as the basis of his conclusions. In the meantime, an additional point should be noted: Miller was no publicity seeker; he did not go off "half cocked." After two years of thorough study he did not rush madly out to proclaim his message to the world. A conservative man by nature, he waited to "double check" every point before making his ideas public.

CHAPTER 4
1818–1831
MILLER AND THE MONOMANIAC

Although Miller had formulated his religious convictions between 1816 and 1818, it was not until the summer of 1831, thirteen years later, that he first presented his ideas publicly. During the intervening years there was little to distinguish him from any other man. He continued to make his living on his farm at Low Hampton. His principal diversion and enjoyment was the study of the Bible.

The conviction that the Lord was soon coming weighed heavily upon his mind, and he was constantly confronted with a question that demanded an answer: In view of his conviction, what was his responsibility to God and to his fellow men; and how could he, an untrained farmer, carry out that responsibility? If the end was as near as he now supposed, it was important that the world should know it. Yet he shrank from the responsibility of making known his convictions.

Various arguments and objections against his beliefs would occur to Miller while he was going about his work. He endeavored to answer all of them from the Bible, "I would not present a view to others while any difficulty appeared to militate against it," he wrote.

Miller was occupied for five years, from 1818 to 1823, weighing the various objections that came to his mind. He said later that no objection was ever presented to him that he had not thought of during that period.

Before 1823 Miller had only thrown out vague hints as to his views, bait at which no one nibbled. But finally he could no longer avoid the responsibility of sharing his convictions with others. In 1823 he began in a definite way to speak of his convictions to his friends, neighbors, ministers, and others whenever he could find or make an opportunity to do so. He was very disappointed to find few who showed any interest at all in what he had to say. Occasionally one would seem to appreciate the force of his argument and the importance of his conclusions, but most people "passed it by as an idle tale."

Believing that the coming of Christ was only a few years away and that this event would determine everyone's eternal destiny, Miller had a natural concern for his relatives and friends. "What are your prospects for eternity?" he asked in a letter to his sister. "That we shall die is certain; and due preparation for a better world is wisdom."

In the same letter, Miller mentioned having attended a dinner in honor of the Marquis de LaFayette, the French hero of the Revolutionary War, who returned to America on a prolonged visit in 1824–1825. That Miller should be invited to attend a dinner in honor of such a renowned figure indicates that he was one of the more prominent and respected citizens of his community.

As time passed, Miller became more and more convinced that he had a personal responsibility to tell others of the nearness of Christ's coming. But he continued to resist the conviction. Like Moses, he shrank from the responsibility and hoped that God would raise up another who would do the work.

But the impression continued: "Go and tell the world: Their blood will I require at thy hand." To satisfy his conscience, he began to speak of his conviction in casual conversations. But the more he did this the more unhappy he became with himself for withholding his message from the public. He told the Lord he was not a speaker, that he was not qualified to hold the attention of an audience. But all his excuses brought no relief.

Miller's teaching that the Second Advent would occur *before* the millennium was much in contrast to the common belief of that day, which was that it would take place *after* a thousand-year period of peace, during which the world would be converted.

The strangeness of Miller's opinion, together with his eagerness to share it with others, naturally caused some comment among the local people. As time passed, his reputation increased in an ever-widening circle. Some of the comments, not all of which were complimentary to his sanity, occasionally reached Miller's ears. It came to his attention one day that a certain doctor in the area had remarked that Mr. Miller was a "fine man," but that he was a monomaniac on the subject of the Second Coming.

Seeing an opportunity to exercise the sense of humor with which he was blessed and at the same time to discuss his favorite subject, Miller decided to have the doctor take his case.

Some time later when one of his children became ill, Miller sent for the doctor. But all the time the doctor was treating the child, Miller sat mutely in a corner of the room, not uttering a word. As Miller had planned, the doctor's curiosity was aroused and he inquired what was wrong. Miller's trap had sprung.

"Well, I hardly know," Miller replied to the doctor's question. "I want you to see what the trouble is and prescribe for me."

The doctor's superficial examination revealed no symptoms. So he asked Miller what *he* thought was wrong.

"I don't know," Miller answered, "but perhaps I am a monomaniac. I want you to examine me and see if I am; and if so, cure me. Can you tell when a man is a monomaniac?"

The doctor blushed at the question, but replied that he thought he could.

"How can you tell?" Miller asked.

"Why, a monomaniac is rational on all subjects but one; and when you talk about that subject, he will react violently."

"In that case," said Miller, "I insist that you see whether or not I am a monomaniac; and if I am, you must cure me. You shall therefore sit down with me for two hours while I present the subject of the Advent to you, and if I am a monomaniac, you will be able to tell it by that time."

When the doctor hesitated, Miller insisted, reminding him that the problem involved Miller's mental health and that therefore the doctor might feel free to make his regular charge for professional services. Unable to find a graceful way out of the situation, the doctor finally consented. So for the next two hours Miller asked questions. And the doctor, under Miller's direction, read the answers from the Bible, in what was probably one of the most unusual "Bible studies" ever given. Before the study was ended, the doctor had been led step by step to the conclusion that Christ was coming to the earth in 1843. At the end of the study he sat back in his chair, paused a moment as if to speak, thought better of it, and without saying another word picked up his hat and left the room.

But the next morning he returned to the Miller home, very much upset.

"Mr. Miller," he said, "I feel that I am going to be lost. I have not slept a wink since I was here yesterday. I have looked at the question from every side, and I cannot see but that the vision *will* end about 1843, and I am not prepared."

So each day for the next week Miller and the doctor spent some time together studying the Bible prophecies. And at the end of the week the doctor was as great a monomaniac as Miller was.

CHAPTER 5
1831–1833
MILLER: A HOUSEHOLD WORD

Fifteen years had passed since Miller, in 1816, had first become convinced that Christ was going to come within his normal life span. And with each passing year the conviction increased that he had a personal responsibility to share his knowledge, not with the few persons who crossed his path, but with the entire world, or with as much of it as he could possibly reach.

It is impossible for us to realize the awfulness of the burden that weighed upon Miller. He was as sure that Christ was going to come in 1843 or 1844 as you are that you are reading these words. He believed that God had given him a message that, if people heard and accepted, would prepare them to meet their Lord in peace. Unwarned, these same people would be eternally lost. The fact that few people seemed ready to accept the message in no way relieved him of his responsibility to preach it. It was his task to sow the seed; it was God's task to reap the harvest.

One Saturday morning in the summer of 1831, Miller sat down as usual to study before he went out in the fields to work. But on that particular morning the conviction came with unusual force, "Go and tell it to the world." The impression came so suddenly and with such force that Miller found himself answering audibly, "I can't go, Lord." A voice seemed to ask, "Why not?" So he recited his excuses: his natural timidity, his lack of ability, and his want of training. But his distress became so great that he found himself saying that if the Lord would open the way by providing an invitation for him to tell about Jesus' coming, he would accept. Immediately the burden was lifted, and he was relieved to think that in all probability he would hear no more about the matter, since he had never received any invitation to present his views.

Miller had not yet learned that man cannot out-bargain God. He did not know that even before he entered into the covenant with God that Saturday morning, God had worked out the arrangements for his first speaking appointment. The invitation was already on its way. For in about half an hour—before Miller had left the room—16-year-old Irving Guilford knocked on the door. Irving was Miller's nephew, the son of his sister Sylvia, and lived in Dresden, about sixteen miles away.

"Uncle William," Irving said, "father sent me over to tell you that our preacher is away, and father wants you to come and talk to the people on the subject of the Lord's coming." Miller thought immediately of the promise he had so recently made to God, and became angry with himself for having made it. Hoping to free himself of his obligation, he abruptly left the room and went to the nearby grove, where he struggled with his conscience for some time. But try as he might, he could not rid himself of the sense of responsibility. At last he promised the Lord that he would go to Dresden if God would give him the grace and the strength that the task required.

Having committed himself again, he returned to the house. Irving was still waiting. After dinner Miller went with him to Dresden. The next day Miller gave his first public discourse on the second coming of Christ. The small building was filled with people eager to hear what he had to say. Once Miller had launched into his subject his timidity left him. Impressed with the importance of his topic, he spoke with unexpected ease.

Thus God arranged that Miller's first public presentation of the Second Advent should be made in the home of Silas and Sylvia Guilford, in Dresden, New York. It was in this little community that two years later Robert G. Ingersoll, who for twenty years was an outspoken enemy of Christianity, was born. Strange indeed are God's ways in the controversy between good and evil!

Miller's message so impressed his audience that they invited him to stay and continue his lectures for a week, which he did. Families came from the surrounding towns and villages, and Miller found himself in the midst of a small revival. "In thirteen families, all but two persons were hopefully converted" to the Second Advent.

When Miller arrived home after his week's stay in Dresden, there was a letter awaiting him from Elder Fuller, of his previous home town, Poultney, Vermont, inviting him to come there and speak in his church. In response to this invitation, Miller gave a series of lectures. Poultney, it will be remembered, was his wife's home town. There she and William had established their first home. So Miller was now presenting his message in home territory to people he knew and who knew him. Christ instructed His first disciples to preach the good news of His first advent "among all nations, beginning at Jerusalem"(Luke 24:47). In the same way, God arranged for Miller to begin preaching the Second Advent in the "Jerusalem" of his own area, among his own relatives, friends, and neighbors. There is no more difficult place to witness than among one's own people. It has always been true that "a prophet is not without honour save in his own country" (Matt. 13:57). Miller stood the test, for in Poultney, as in Dresden, there were converts to his teaching. He was especially encouraged when Elder Fuller became his first convert from within the ministry.

Miller's lectures at Dresden and Poultney were but the introduction to a new way of life that was to continue for many years. In a short time he was receiving more invitations than he could fill. Never again, as long as he lived, was he without an opportunity to speak.

One of the first ministers to befriend Miller was Elder Truman Hendryx, a Baptist, whom he met first in the summer of 1831, shortly before Miller gave his lectures at Dresden. The two men became good friends, and over the years carried on a correspondence that has become the source of much information on Miller's life and work.

Hendryx has recorded the circumstances under which he first met Miller. Because of his eagerness to talk about the Second Advent and his ability to defend his views on that subject, Miller had by 1831 become somewhat of a local celebrity among the churchgoing people around Low Hampton. As a result, some people, even among the ministers, were reluctant to enter into any discussion with him. Hendryx had heard that Miller was "hard on ministers who differed with him," so it was with a certain degree of fear and trembling that he called on Miller at the request of his superior church officer.

But he discovered that his fear of meeting Miller was groundless. Instead of pouncing upon him like a tiger, as Hendryx had expected, Miller treated him with extreme kindness.

In one of his early letters to Hendryx, Miller wrote about a certain Brother Sawyer who shared some of Miller's views but who had "not improved so much in Bible knowledge as he might" because he "was afraid of being a Millerite." This statement is of some significance, for it contains the first known use of the term *Millerite*. It was not long before the term became a household word, often to be used in contempt and ridicule.

Elders Fuller and Hendryx were not the only ministers who heard of Miller's unusual teaching. In a letter written in the spring of 1832, Miller told of a young minister who visited his home "on purpose to learn these strange notions of `crazy Miller's,' or at least to save Brother Miller, if possible, from going down to the grave with such error." Although the two men had never met before, the young man stayed several days in Miller's home, studying the Bible "night and day" while Miller "held the concordance."

While Miller eventually spoke to audiences numbering in the thousands, he always had a deep respect for the one-soul audience. Much of his time was spent in working on a person-to-person basis. In fact, he was convinced that many times the minister can do more while working on a one-to-one relationship than he can in any other way. People expect the minister to preach from the pulpit, he reasoned; it is the work for which he is paid. But when he visits with an individual "by the fireside" the minister must be motivated by a love for that person's soul. The result is often more effective than that of formal preaching.

During the summer of 1832 Miller and several of his neighbors began to meet in the local schoolhouse at five o'clock in the morning to pray for the Second Advent and an outpouring of the Holy Spirit. Although this practice was not continued indefinitely, it was in a way symbolic of the dedication and enthusiasm that later came to characterize the Millerite movement.

Soon after Miller began his public lectures he sent to the local newspaper a series of articles in which he presented his views on the Second Advent. But because he had not signed the articles, the editor, in harmony with common practice, refused to publish them. But a short time later there did appear a series of sixteen articles over the initials W. M. The first article appeared May 15, 1832. It is possible that Miller had written the original material before he began to present his views publicly, in an attempt to satisfy his conscience. Or he may have written it soon after he began his preaching, in response to requests that he put his ideas into print. Whatever the circumstances, the articles appeared less than a year after he began his public work.

The Universalist doctrine was popular during the 1800's, but Miller had no sympathy with that belief. The idea that eventually everyone will be saved he found contrary to the teaching of the Bible. Because one of his sisters was married to a Universalist, he frequently expressed his concern in his correspondence with her.

In a letter written in the spring of 1832, Miller cautioned his brother-in-law not to be deceived by the Universalist belief, for, Miller warned, "the time is shortly coming that will try every man's work, whether it be good or evil." He continued by pointing out that if it is true that all men will be saved, as the Universalist believe, it is too bad that Paul didn't know it when he wrote that he might save "some" (1 Cor. 9:22), when he should have said—according to Miller's brother-in-law—that "all" would be saved. Miller pointed out that much argument and misunderstanding would have been avoided if Paul, Peter, the writers of the Gospels, and even Christ Himself, had said nothing about there being two classes of mankind, the sheep and the goats, and nothing about everlasting punishment. Then with a touch of irony,

Miller suggested that of course the Universalists were wiser than the Bible writers.

By February, 1833, there were at least nine ministers who were preaching Miller's belief in regard to the Second Advent, "more or less," as Miller said. Some accepted his basic premise but differed with him in varying degrees on the details. One of these believing ministers was a young Congregational preacher, Henry Jones, who wrote to Miller early in 1833. He had an inquiring mind and at one time or another was affiliated with temperance and antislavery movements. He became interested in the Millerite movement through reading some of Miller's articles and talking with another minister about the millennium. He became very interested in studying the book of Revelation and read and reread it many times. In 1834 he wrote to Miller that he had memorized the complete book. Jones became a leader in the movement and was one who, with Miller, Himes, and others, signed the official call for the holding of the first general conference of Adventists in 1840.

In 1833 the Baptist church of which Miller was a member first considered issuing him a license to preach. He was one week away from his fifty-first birthday. He was "too old, too wicked, too proud" to deserve the privilege of such a license he wrote Elder Hendryx. But the license was granted on September 14, 1833. Two days later he wrote to his sister, "My brethren have given me a license—unworthy and old and disobedient as I am. Oh, to grace how great a debtor!"

Because Miller now carried a license to preach, Elder Hendryx in his next letter addressed him as "*Rev.* William Miller." But Miller would have none of it.

Always one to come straight to the point, Miller in his reply suggested that Hendryx take his Bible and "see if you can find the word `Rev.' applied to a sinful mortal as myself; and govern yourself accordingly." Miller went on to say that he was interested only in "Jesus, and a knowledge of his word, faith in his name, hope in his grace, interest in his love," not in "high-sounding titles."

In 1833 Miller published his views in a sixty-four-page pamphlet. With the exception of the sixteen articles that had appeared in the *Telegraph* the year before and which had a very limited circulation, this was the first publishing of his ideas for the public. It was the beginning of a great flood of printed matter that was to be published by the Millerites during the next twelve years.

Shortly after he published the pamphlet, while visiting New York City, Miller was a passenger on a boat on the Hudson River. Near him was a group of men who were commenting on the wonderful scientific progress that had been made during the preceding thirty years. One of them expressed the opinion that such progress could not possibly continue, or "man will be something more than human." Alert to every opportunity to preach the message, Miller replied that conditions reminded him of Daniel 12:4—"Many shall run to and fro, and knowledge shall be increased." Then, taking advantage of the pause that followed, he gave his listeners an informal lecture on the eleventh chapter of Daniel. The men listened with close attention. When he had finished his comments Miller remarked apologetically that he had not intended to infringe so long upon their time and patience. Then he left them and walked to the other end of the boat. But the entire group followed him and asked to hear more. Miller discussed with them the second, seventh, eighth, and ninth chapters of Daniel. At the conclusion of his study the men asked whether he had any literature they might take with them. In response to their request he gave them all the copies of the pamphlet that he had with him.

In a letter written in the spring of 1833 Miller reaffirmed his faith in the Bible as the Word of God:

> It tells us what we were, are, and shall be; begins with the beginning, carries us through the intermediate, and ends only with the end; it is past, present and to come; it discovers the first great cause;…it speaks of life, death, and judgment, body, soul and spirit, heaven, earth and hell; it makes use of all nature as figures, to sum up the value of the gospel; it declares itself to be the WORD OF GOD. And your friend and brother believes it.[1]

---

1 *A Brief History of William Miller*, 126

Because he kept no record of the places he visited before October, 1834, it is impossible to trace Miller's movements in detail. But, beginning at a place that he called "The Forks," which is generally assumed to be Mooer's Forks in Clinton County, New York, he recorded in two small black books the places he visited, with the dates and the texts from which he preached. He referred to these as his "text books."

Two years had passed since Miller had entered into his covenant with God. The first lecture at Dresden had been multiplied many times during the intervening two years. In the fall of 1833 one of Miller's friends wrote that "The name of Wm. Miller is a household word throughout the world."

It is difficult to determine accurately how many Millerites or Adventists there were at any given time. Those who separated from other churches to join the movement were relatively easy to identify, but many Millerites retained membership in their churches. They maintained their belief in Adventism, but chose to carry on their work within the framework of organized religious bodies. Because of this, they were difficult to identify with certainty. In 1845, looking back on the movement after the Disappointment, Miller wrote that he could account for "some fifty thousand believers" in "a thousand advent congregations." Miller never made extravagant claims regarding the number of Adventists. His figure is probably conservative. He also estimated that "about two hundred ministers" and "about five hundred public lecturers" had embraced and proclaimed his view. "Ministers" were those who had some bona fide ministerial background in an organized church before they joined the Millerite movement. "Public lecturers" were spokesmen for the movement who came from other professions or trades, without ministerial background. That two hundred ministers would give up their pulpits and jeopardize their ministerial standing to join the unpopular Advent Movement is nothing short of remarkable. It indicates the convicting power that attended the movement.

The first serious attempt to determine the number of Adventists in the United States was made by E. T. Taylor in 1860. At that time, sixteen years after the Disappointment, there were, according to his figures, fifty thousand who remained loyal to their Adventist beliefs in spite of the disappointments. Millerite Adventism reached its peak during the summer of 1844, when fifty thousand Millerites came out of other churches to join the movement.² Some authorities place the number of Millerites in the United States at that time at two hundred thousand, which is probably as accurate a figure as we can arrive at.³

This figure may not appear impressive today when we number the population of some of our larger cities in the millions. But it becomes more meaningful when we realize that the total population of the United States in 1840 was only a little more than seventeen million.⁴ If we accept the figure of two hundred thousand Adventists, we must conclude that in the United States approximately one person out of every eighty-five was a Millerite.

The number of Millerites outside the United States is difficult to determine. But it is evident that in England the movement made considerable impact. In May, 1843, *The Midnight Cry* reported that 15,000 copies of certain Millerite books were being printed, and that "Methodists, Baptists, and Independent preachers have embraced the doctrine, and are at work."⁵

In the January, 1844, issue of the same paper it was reported that "the Advent doctrine is chiefly the talk in this country now....Thousands are now looking for the coming of the Lord, and believe it is at the door....The midnight cry has produced such powerful effects in some parts of this country, that nearly whole villages have turned to the Lord....Our Norfolk mission is doing exceedingly well. Near one thousand have embraced this doctrine in Norfolk of late."

---

2 Ellen G. White, *The Great Controversy* (Mountain View, California: Pacific Press Publishing Association, 1950), 376.

3 Figures quoted by Dr. David T. Arthur, chairman of the division of humanities, Aurora College, Aurora, Illinois, and authority on the Millerite movement, in a lecture at Loma Linda University, April 20, 1973.

4 U.S. Bureau of the Census, quoted from *Information Please Almanac* (New York: Simon and Schuster, 1973).

5 Francis D. Nichol, *The Midnight Cry* (Washington, D.C.: Review and Herald Publishing Association, 1944), p. 142.

"The advent movement of 1840–44 was a glorious manifestation of the power of God; the first angel's message was carried to every mission station in the world, and in some countries there was the greatest religious interest which has been witnessed...since the Reformation of the sixteenth century."[6]

Factors that we shall discuss briefly in the next chapter called attention to Miller's message, bolstered the faith of many people in its truthfulness, and helped to swell the movement's ranks.

---

6   *The Great Controversy*, p. 611.

CHAPTER 6
1833-1840
A NEW ERA

Few things did more to attract attention to the fulfillment of Bible prophecy and thus to give impetus to Miller's cause than two astronomical phenomena that occurred during the 1830's and 1840's. Although the second event does not fall within the time span covered in this chapter, because of their celestial relationship we shall discuss them both here.

In the early morning hours of November 13, 1833, an unusually large meteoric shower covered much of North America. Commonly referred to as "the falling of the stars," it was especially heavy in the Northeastern States, the very area where the Millerite movement originated and exerted its greatest influence. This was the most extensive and wonderful display of falling stars that has ever been recorded. Thousands of people viewed this event as a direct fulfillment of Bible prophecy, a sign of the nearness of the second coming of Christ. (See Gen. 1:14; Matt. 24:6, 9; Rev. 6:13.) To the Millerites especially the "falling of the stars" was significant, and many non-Millerites were constrained to regard Miller's teaching in a more serious light than before.

The second phenomenon occurred about ten years later, when from February 28 to April 1, 1843, the night sky was lighted with the most brilliant comet to appear in the nineteenth century. Called the "Great Comet of 1843," it should not be confused with Halley's Comet, which is better known but which was less brilliant. To the serious-minded, it seemed again as if the very heavens were proclaiming the Second Advent. It appeared to them that nature was confirming what the Bible taught and what the Millerites already believed.

But more than either the falling of the stars or the appearance of the Great Comet, a direct fulfillment of Bible prophecy in 1840 inspired faith in the Scriptures as the word of God and strengthened the position of the Millerite movement. In 1838 a Millerite preacher, Josiah Litch, wrote a series of articles on the seven trumpets of Revelation 8 and 9. He stated that the sixth trumpet would cease to sound on August 11, 1840, and that the independence of the Ottoman Empire as such would cease to exist after that date. When this happened, he said, the world could know without a doubt that a day in prophecy represents a year, as Miller and his followers taught. Such a startling and definite prediction—naming the specific day—naturally attracted wide attention. People began to look to Turkey, the center of the Ottoman Empire, with new interest.

Although in the past there had been serious difficulty between the pasha of Egypt and the sultan of Turkey, the tension had eased by 1838. War between the two countries seemed unlikely when Litch published his prediction. But in 1839 the two countries did go to war, which dragged on into 1840. Then the allied powers of England, Russia, Austria, and Prussia intervened and offered an ultimatum to the Turkish sultan. In the words of Dr. Jerome Clark, "By accepting the intervention of the allied powers to bring a settlement of his difficulties with Egypt's pasha, the Ottoman Turkish sultan had lost control of his external affairs insofar as Egypt was concerned....The pasha took the message under advisement on August 11, 1840. That same day the sultan wrote the four powers for assurances of their help should the ultimatum be refused. Turkey from that time forward was known as the 'sick man of Europe.' The pasha complied with the ultimatum. The prophecy of the 1,391 years and fifteen days of Ottoman Turkish domination had been fulfilled to the day."[1] The event exactly fulfilled the prediction.

The literal fulfillment of this Bible prophecy made a deep impression upon thousands of people. Josiah Litch reported that within a few months after August 11, 1840, more than a thousand former infidels wrote him saying they had been led to accept the Bible as the word of God. Some of these later became preachers in the Millerite movement.

1   Jerome L. Clark, *1844*, 3 vols. (Nashville: Southern Publishing Association, 1968), vol. 1, 34, 35.

Considering these factors—the "falling stars," the Great Comet, the fulfillment of prophecy—all of which were associated in the minds of the public with the Millerite movement, and remembering that Miller himself was the personification of the movement, it is not difficult to believe that it was almost literally true that Miller's name was a "household word" throughout the United States and in other parts of the world.

There were of course some communities and churches that did not welcome Miller or his message. Some ministers warned their congregations to stay away from his meetings, with the result that in many cases people went to them to satisfy their aroused curiosity. After delivering his first lecture in one town, Miller received a letter signed by ten "bullies and blackguards" saying that if he did not get out of the State they would put him where even the dogs would not be able to find him. But Miller was not a man to cower before a threat. He stayed; he delivered his lectures; and God blessed his work in that community.

Some people sincerely felt it was their duty to discourage Miller in his work. Often these were people who had not attended any of his lectures and whose convictions were therefore based on hearsay and rumor. Noah Webster, for instance, wrote to Miller, "Your preaching can be of no use to society but it is a great annoyance. If you expect to frighten men and women into religion, you are probably mistaken.... If your preaching drives people into despair or insanity, you are responsible for the consequences. I advise you to abandon your preaching; you are doing no good, but you may do a great deal of harm."[2] But Miller took his marching orders from God, not from Webster. He was no more to be stopped by Webster's reasoning than he was by the bullies' threatenings.

Miller's time was becoming more and more occupied with lecturing and other matters related to his sharing his conviction with the public. In a letter written to his friend Hendryx in October, 1834, he related that in a six-week period he had given thirty-six lectures on Christ's second coming,

---

2   Arthur W. Spalding, *Origin and History of Seventh-day Adventists* (Washington, D.C.: Review and Herald Publishing Association, 1961), 53.

attended four meetings, two of which were protracted, and worked with a number of new converts.

With the busy schedule Miller set for himself, it is easy to lose sight of the fact that his lecturing was only a part-time job. His and his family's living depended upon his work on the farm. And with eight children, this was no small responsibility.

The Baptist Church had granted him a license to preach, but this did not carry with it any financial remuneration. Not until he took a short trip into Canada in 1835 did he receive his first donation—the sum of one dollar—to help defray the expenses of the trip. But the increasing number of speaking appointments began to leave little time for farming, and he had to make a decision whether to farm or to lecture; he could no longer do both. So, near the close of 1834, he "let out" his farm to one of his sons. At the same time he wrote to Hendryx, "I devote my whole time, lecturing." It appears that he also resigned from his duties as a justice of the peace at about the same time he quit farming.

In a letter to Hendryx, Miller wrote that "Old Elder Fuller is preaching this same doctrine in Connecticut and writes me that it has a powerful effect." This was the same Elder Fuller who had invited Miller to speak at Dresden "on the subject of the Lord's coming," and who had been among Miller's first converts.

Miller spent the first week of January, 1835, lecturing in Addison, Vermont, and the second week in Cornwall. Then he returned to his home, where he stayed until the middle of February. By this time quite a large number of ministers of the Baptist Church had heard his sermons. Several of them went on record as endorsing his work by issuing him a certificate to preach.

This certificate, issued March 19, 1835, was granted in addition to the one that had been issued previously in the fall of 1833, which Miller still carried.

After lecturing in several of the surrounding towns during May and June, Miller embarked on a tour into lower Canada. It was after one of his lectures on this tour that a woman pressed two half-dollars into his hand as he greeted her at the door after the lecture. This was the first financial assistance he received. Until then, all the expenses of his travels had been paid from his own pocket.

While returning from Canada he felt impressed to go to his home as quickly as possible. So strong was this impression that he canceled several speaking appointments and took the shortest route home, expecting some member of the family to be ill or in trouble. He was greatly relieved to find everything quite normal when he arrived on a Sunday evening. Early the next morning he went to see his mother, who lived about half a mile away with another son, Solomon. Miller had a gift for her that he had brought from one of his sisters who lived in Canada and whom he had visited on his trip. He spent almost the entire day with his mother.

Soon after he returned to his own home she suffered a stroke and lost her power of speech. Solomon sent for him, and he returned immediately to her bedside. By the pressure of her hand she indicated that she recognized him. But she passed away before the end of the week. Miller often expressed his appreciation of that last visit with his mother, which would not have been possible had he not followed the sudden urge to change his plans and return home immediately. He always gratefully regarded the impelling impression as coming from God. His mother had not accepted his teachings, but she encouraged him to preach the truth as he believed it.

On June 19, 1835, Miller visited Lansingburgh, New York, where he lectured through the twenty-sixth. To help defray the cost of his stage fare someone gave him four dollars. This, with the two half-dollars given him in Canada, was all the financial remuneration he had received to that time. His public work was never any financial advantage to him, contrary to what some people preferred to believe. The result was that his personal property and fortune, small to begin with, gradually diminished during his public ministry.

'Referring to his work in Lansingburgh, Miller wrote that his lectures were well received, and that people of various persuasions—infidels, deists, Universalists, and Sectarians—listened to hear him, "the stammering old man," talk about the second coming of Christ. "It was only God," he wrote, "who could produce such an effect on an audience."

By April, 1836, Miller could name eight Baptist ministers who were preaching his views, and in a letter to Hendryx he added, "Many others believe but dare not preach it." Not often do ministers change their religious beliefs. But there was in Miller's message a convicting power that caused preachers to accept his teaching and espouse his cause even at the cost of their pulpits. That these ministers were not deluded by trickery, overwhelmed by oratory, or subjected to emotional appeals, is evidenced by the fact that several of them were converted to Miller's cause without ever having heard him speak. They were convinced of the truth by reading his writings. Charles Fitch, about whom we shall hear later, is an example of one who was convicted by reading.

On the twenty-third of January, 1837, Miller began a series of sixteen lectures in Shaftsbury, Vermont. At the close of one of the lectures an Elder Mattison, a Baptist minister, arose and asked permission to speak. Permission being granted, he said he had come to the meetings with the purpose of exposing the folly of Mr. Miller, but that he had been "convicted, confounded, and converted." He had, he said, applied some uncomplimentary names to Mr. Miller, such as "the-end-of-the-world man," "dreamer," and "fanatic," for which he then apologized publicly. The apparent sincerity of the man produced a solemn effect upon the audience.

Records reveal no additional unusual experience during the rest of 1837. Miller continued to present his lectures without incident, and nothing would be added to this narrative by detailing the various places he visited.

In the early spring of 1838 Miller received a letter from a clergyman who was later to become one of the three most prominent leaders in the Millerite movement. It read as follows:

Boston, March 5, 1838

> MY DEAR BROTHER: I am the pastor of an Orthodox Congregational Church in this city. A few weeks since [i.e., ago] your lectures on the second coming of Christ were put into my hands. I sat down to read the work, know-

ing nothing of the views which it contained. I have studied it with an overwhelming interest, such as I never felt in any other book except the Bible. I have compared it with Scripture and history, and I find nothing on which to rest a single doubt respecting the correctness of your views. Though a miserable, guilty sinner, I trust that, through the Lord's abounding grace, I shall be among those that "love his appearing." I preached to my people two discourses yesterday on the coming of our Lord, and I believe a deep and permanent interest will be awakened thereby, in God's testimonies.

Yours in the faith of Jesus Christ,
CHARLES FITCH[3]

This was the first direct communication between Miller and Fitch, who had "read his way" into the Millerite movement. But this letter was the beginning of an association that, with only one brief interruption, was to continue until Fitch's death in October of 1844.

Fitch began to preach Miller's views in the early months of 1838. However, he was extremely disappointed when many of his fellow clergymen not only failed to accept them but made them the object of their ridicule and contempt. Because of this he gave up his newly accepted teachings. But about three years later, encouraged by Josiah Litch, about whom we shall have more to say, Fitch again embraced Miller's views. From that time until his death he was one of the movement's most enthusiastic and aggressive leaders. Not only was he a gifted speaker but he made several other valuable contributions to the movement. With Apollo's Hale he originated the well-known prophetic chart, used by several of the early Adventist pioneers.

In January, 1843, Fitch began to publish a weekly paper called the *Second Advent of Christ*. In the issue of July 26, 1843, he printed a sermon on Revelation 14 and 18. In this sermon he presented the idea that the term *Babylon* included not only the Roman Catholic Church but also the main body of Protestant churches, which by that time had rejected the doctrine of the Second Advent. This broader application of "Babylon" was eventually accepted by the Millerites and

3 *Brief History of William Miller*, 140, 141.

many of their spiritual descendants, including Seventh-day Adventists.

But we are ahead of our story, and must return to the spring of 1838. By that time Miller was receiving more invitations to speak than he could possibly accept. Many of these requests came through the mail from pastors whom he had not met but who had heard of him. One such letter, flavored with a touch of humor, will serve as an example of many that Miller received.

Rome, N.Y., March 20, 1838

> DEAR BROTHER MILLER:...We have heard something of you and yours, and want to see you here in person, and hear your whole course of lectures. I feel as if the time had arrived for you "to preach the Gospel at Rome also."[4]

And so Miller went to Rome, New York, where he lectured from May 6 through 16. In June he made another tour into Canada. He had also received a letter from an Elder T. Cole, inviting him to lecture in the city of Lowell, Massachusetts, and plans were made accordingly. On the day appointed, Elder Cole went to the railroad station to meet Miller. The two men had not met, and neither knew what the other looked like. It happened that Miller's attire was often more appropriate for his former occupation as a farmer than as a public lecturer. But Elder Cole, judging from the reports he had heard regarding the success of Miller's meetings elsewhere, expected him to be dressed like the proverbial doctor of divinity of that time. Cole watched closely as the passengers alighted from the train, but he saw no one who fitted the appearance he had conjured up of the man he expected to meet. At last he spotted a man who was shaking a bit from the palsy, and wearing a white hat and a camlet coat. Hoping that this was not his man, but fearing that it was, and if so, regretting that he had asked him to lecture in his church, Cole approached and asked, "Is your name Miller?"

Miller nodded that it was.

"Well," said Cole, "follow me."

---

4 Ibid., 142.

Cole led the way, with Miller keeping up as best he could, until they reached the Cole home. Cole was embarrassed to think that he had gotten himself into such a situation. Judging from appearances, he was sure this man could know little of the Bible. But there seemed to be no way out of the situation. The meeting had been announced, and he must make the best of what obviously was going to be a bad situation. After the evening meal, Cole waited as long as he dared, dreading to face what he knew had to be faced. But at last he announced that it was time to go to the church. Again they walked, with Cole leading the way and Miller bringing up the rear. When the time for the meeting arrived, Cole showed Miller into the pulpit, but, wanting to be as inconspicuous as possible in what he was sure was going to be a miniature catastrophe, found a seat for himself in the congregation.

Alone on the rostrum, Miller read a hymn and asked the congregation to sing it. Then he offered prayer and read another hymn, which was also sung. He felt ill at ease at being alone in a strange pulpit. But he launched into his subject, taking as his text Titus 2:13, "Looking for that blessed hope, and the glorious appearing of the great God and our Saviour Jesus Christ." He soon lost himself in his subject and forgot the awkwardness of the situation.

After a few minutes had passed, Cole saw that he had drastically underrated both Miller's knowledge of the Bible and his ability as a public speaker. Leaving his place in the congregation, he took his seat on the platform.

Miller continued his lectures in Lowell from the fourteenth to the twenty-second of May, 1839, and, in spite of what had begun as a very awkward situation, returned only a week later to begin a second series, from May 29 to June 4. The conclusion of the story is much happier than its beginning. Not only did Elder Cole himself embrace Miller's views "in full" but on July 25 he wrote to Miller that he had "baptized about forty, sixty in all having joined the church; and there are yet some who are seeking the Lord."

And that was not all, for Miller recorded that "at Lowell I also became acquainted with my Bro. J. Litch, who had previously embraced my views, and who has since so aided their extension by his faithful lectures and writings, and energetic and consistent course." It appears that this was the first time Miller and Litch, who had "read himself into the movement," met each other.

Miller's friend, Hendryx, invited him to speak at his church in Pennsylvania, assuring him of a full house. Miller wrote in reply that he did not need to go there to see a church not only crammed but jammed. For the preceding Sunday he had preached in a church that was jammed full, lobby and all. But Miller stated that that did not give him special pleasure; the multitude that may today cry Hosanna in your honor, may tomorrow cry Crucify him!

Few things reveal one's personality and character more truthfully than the letters one writes. Miller's letters indicate that he was a clear-thinking man, with a good understanding of human nature; that he had an unusual knowledge of Bible prophecy, and a generous amount of humor. But, in common with most leaders, he had moments of self-doubt. On one occasion, for example, he wrote to his friend Hendryx that there were times when he felt as though he could do all things through Christ; but there were other times when "the shaking of a leaf" brought terror to his heart, and he was impressed with his own inadequacy.

Miller also wrote to Hendryx of having received a letter from a certain Elder West who vigorously took him to task for preaching error on certain matters; and of also having received a letter from an Elder Claflin, who just as vigorously charged him with preaching the opposite view on the same matter! And Miller observed that "they both quote Bible" to support their position!

Such situations caused Miller to evaluate his own positions and lines of reasoning very carefully, for he recognized that there was always the possibility of error in his own conclusions.

The only way he could avoid this possibility, he concluded, was to do his best with God's help to divest himself of all preconceived ideas, continue to read the Bible for himself, use his God-given judgment, preach what he believed to be the truth, and leave the results in God's hands. What more can anyone do than this?

Another letter, written to his oldest son, serves as a small window through which we may catch an additional glimpse of the personality that was Miller. Convinced that of himself he had neither the power of mind nor the strength of body to do what he was doing, he could only conclude that the Lord was using him as His instrument; that it was really God who through him was warning men of their danger. Then, voicing the burden that has been carried by concerned Christians in every place and at every time, he pleaded with the Lord to "awake the people of God in Hampton"—his friends and neighbors—"who are sleeping over the volcano of God's wrath."

Miller lectured in Groton, Massachusetts, from May 24 to 28, and in Lynn from June 3 to 9, when he concluded his tour into that State. He then summed up his work of the past several years with this entry in his journal: "Thus ends my tour into Massachusetts, making eight hundred lectures from October 1, 1834, to June 9, 1839—four years, six months, and nine days."

This entry concludes Miller's first "Text Book." The second continues the record into 1844. Together, they give evidence of the untiring labor he performed during the decade they cover.

Following Miller's lectures in Lynn, the editor of the Lynn Record commented that the lecturer pretended to be nothing more than a plain farmer who had studied Bible prophecies intensely for a number of years, who understood the prophecies differently from most people, and who wanted to share his views with as many people as possible. The editor added that no one, after listening to Miller for five minutes, could doubt his sincerity.

Not all articles appearing in the public press were as kind in their treatment of Miller as this, however. As 1843—the year of the expected Advent—drew closer, the news media in general became, with few exceptions, more unsympathetic, hostile, and abusive. False rumors arose with increasing frequency, as they often do concerning controversial figures. The report was circulated that Miller was "making a fortune" from his lectures when in reality he was taking money from his own small savings to finance his work. A rumor was circulated that he had died. No sooner was this squelched than there went out another to the effect that he had reexamined his calculations and discovered that he had made an error of one hundred years. Reports such as these were repeatedly revived.

Returning to his home following his work in Lynn, Miller gave his lectures in several of the smaller towns in the area surrounding Low Hampton. At Colchester, Vermont, twenty-three new members were added to the Baptist church before the end of the year, directly or indirectly attributable to his meetings.

Meetings Miller conducted at Exeter proved to be most important in their influence on the Millerite movement. During the meetings, a conference of the Christian Connection was held in the city, and some of the participants took the opportunity to call on him. It was on this occasion that Miller first met Joshua V. Himes, pastor of the Chardon Street church in Boston. Himes had previously written to Miller, inviting him to lecture in his church. At Exeter, the invitation was renewed, with the result that Miller went to Boston on the seventh of December and lectured in Himes's church from the eighth to the sixteenth.

During this time Miller was a guest in Himes home. This provided ample opportunity for the two men to discuss Miller's ideas and plans for the future. Before Miller had progressed very far in his series Himes had accepted his views regarding the nature and the nearness of the Second Advent, although he had some reservations about the exact time. But before the lectures came to a close Himes was convinced of the truthfulness of Miller's message and had begun to take a great interest in its promulgation.

"When Mr. Miller had closed his lectures," recounted Himes later, "I found myself in a new position. I could not believe or preach as I had done. Light on this subject was blazing on my conscience day and night. A long conversation with Mr. Miller then took place, on our duties and responsibilities. I said to Bro. Miller, 'Do you really believe this doctrine?'

"He replied, 'I certainly do, or I would not preach it.'

"'What are you doing to spread or diffuse it through the world?'

"'I have done and am still doing all I can.'

"'Well, the whole thing is kept in a corner yet. There is but little knowledge on the subject, after all you have done. If Christ is to come in a few years, as you believe, no time should be lost in giving the church and world warning, in thundertones, to arouse them to prepare.'

"'I know it, I know it, Bro. Himes,' said he; 'but what can an old farmer do? I was never used to public speaking; I stand quite alone; and, though I have labored much, and seen many converted to God and the truth, yet *no one*, as yet, seems to enter into the *object* and *spirit of my mission*, so as to render me much aid. They like to have me preach, and build up their churches; and there it ends, with most of the ministers, as yet. I have been looking for help—I want help.'

"It was at this time that I laid myself, family, society, reputation, all upon the altar of God, to help him, to the extent of my power, to the end. I then inquired of him what parts of the country he had visited, and whether he had visited any of our principal cities."

Miller told him of his labors which, as we have seen, had up to that time been limited largely to the towns and smaller cities of a relatively small area.

"'But why,' I said, 'have you not gone into the large cities?'

"He replied that his rule was to visit those places, where invited, and that he had not been invited into any of the large cities.

"'Well,' said I, 'will you go with me where doors are opened?'

"'Yes, I am ready to go anywhere, and labor to the extent of my ability to the end.'

"I then told him he might prepare for the campaign; for doors should be opened in every city in the Union, and the warning should go to the ends of the earth. Here I began to 'help' Father Miller."

God in His providence had brought the two men together. The beginning of this association opened a new era in Miller's work of spreading his convictions regarding the soon-coming Christ.

Miller was a product of the frontier country, so it is not strange that he hesitated to enter the large cities, with which he had no contact and with whose ways he was unfamiliar. Rather, it is to be marveled at that he had accomplished as much as he did. But with the new association, Miller's message moved out of the villages and hamlets into the nation's more populous centers. For while Miller remained the movement's chief spokesman, Himes soon became its main promoter. He became publicity director, propagandist, and advance man, arranging speaking appointments for Miller in some of the country's largest and most expensive halls and auditoriums. It was largely Himes's work that caused the influence of Millerism to expand rapidly within the next few months.

Himes did not associate himself with Miller without first counting the cost. Writing of this, Himes stated:

> We are not insensible of the fact, that much obloquy will be cast upon us in consequence of our association with the author of this work [Miller]. This, however, gives us no pain. We had rather be associated with such a man as William Miller, and stand with him in gloom or glory, in the cause of the living God, than to be associated with his enemies, and enjoy all the honors of this world.[5]

Thus it was that Joshua V. Himes, scarcely thirty-five years old, gave up a promising future to cast his lot with an unpopular cause. But Himes was no stranger to unpopular causes. He was an energetic opponent of the liquor traffic, and for a time he had worked closely with William Lloyd Garrison in the battle against slavery. As pastor of the Chardon Street Chapel, he had opened the doors of the church to more than one reform cause. Millerism was therefore only one of

---

5   Ibid., 148.

several "causes" with which Himes was actively associated. But it was the one to which he was to devote the most time and effort. And, with Miller and Fitch, he became one of Millerism's three leading figures.

Himes was a speaker of unusual ability, and he frequently lectured on the subject of the Second Advent. But his most important contribution to the movement was in the field of organization and promotion. He published charts, pamphlets, tracts, songbooks, broadsides, and handbills. At different times he published no less than half a dozen periodicals devoted to promoting the teaching of the Second Advent. One of his first acts after associating himself with Miller was to arrange for the printing of five thousand copies of Miller's revised *Lectures*. As Miller supplied the fuel of the Advent movement, so Himes supplied the spark the movement needed.

In the middle of December, 1839, after he had concluded his meetings in Himes's church, Miller lectured in Westford, Massachusetts, where he was refused the use of the Congregational church. This was the first time a church was closed to him. However, this refusal did not greatly hinder the work.

On January 21, 1840, Miller began his lectures in Portsmouth, New Hampshire. Among those who attended the series was an Elder D. I. Robinson, pastor of the Methodist church. Robinson was a doubter of Miller's teaching and like some others was determined to "set Miller straight." But he hesitated to do it publicly, lest as he says, "evil should follow." So, arming himself with a list of objections, he visited Miller privately. He was surprised that none of his objections were new to Miller, who answered them as fast as he could present them. Robinson went home "used up, convicted, humbled, and resolved to examine the question" again. Having done so, he began to preach the message Miller was preaching.

From February 8 to 29, Miller gave his third series of lectures in the city of Boston. It was toward the end of this series, on February 28, 1840, that Himes brought out the first issue of a paper devoted to spreading the Advent doctrine, the *Signs of the Times*.

Most papers, both religious and secular, had become quite unsympathetic in their treatment of Miller and his message. And almost no papers would print anything from him in rebuttal. For some time he had wished for a periodical that would serve as a voice of Millerism. But, as he later wrote, "we had never been able to find a man who was willing to run the risk of his reputation and pecuniary expense, in such a publication." But when Miller expressed his desires to Himes, he accepted the challenge. It was typical of the energetic Himes that he brought out the first issue of the paper the very next week, without a single subscriber or the promise of financial assistance from anyone. And with the publication of the *Signs*, as the paper was commonly called, there began a new era for the expanding Millerite movement.

In 1844 the name of Himes's paper was changed to the *Advent Herald*. Thirty years later, when James White began to publish a weekly paper to speak for the Seventh-day Adventists on the Pacific Coast, he adopted the name that Himes had abandoned, and called his paper the *Signs of the Times*. However, White's paper was not a descendant or continuation of Himes's; there was no connection between the two except in name. *The Signs* begun by White is still published at Mountain View, California.

The phrase "signs of the times" was so significant to the people of White's day that several papers were given the name. In addition to the two already mentioned, the Latter-Day Saints (Mormons), who arose at approximately the same time as the Millerites, also chose *Signs of the Times* as the name of one of their publications.

From Boston, Miller went to Watertown, Massachusetts, on the first of March, 1840. He was very pleased with the way things went there, and wrote to his son, "I have never seen so great an effect in any one place as there. I preached...from Gen. xix.17. There were from a thousand to fifteen hundred present, and more than one hundred under conviction." In commenting on the Watertown meetings, the *Signs of the Times* stated it was not so much the belief that Christ was coming in 1843 that led to conviction, as it was the certainty of His coming at some time in the near future, and the realization that they were not prepared to greet His coming with joy.

From March 11 to 23, Miller presented his first series of lectures in the Christian church of Portland, Maine. As usual, the influence of the Holy Spirit was felt, and lives were changed. One pastor reported:

> There has probably never been so much religious interest among the inhabitants of this place, generally, as at present. A number of rum-sellers have turned their shops into meeting-rooms; and those places that were once devoted to intemperance and revelry are now devoted to prayer and praise. There is nothing like extravagant excitement, but an almost universal solemnity on the minds of all the people. One of the principal book-sellers informed me that he had sold more Bibles in *one month*, since Mr. Miller came here, than he had in any four months previous.[6]

One young man, hardly more than a boy, heard about Miller's meetings. Although he was not a Christian, he decided he would hear what Miller had to say. But first he went to a saloon where a dozen or so of his friends were playing cards. He invited them to leave their gambling and to go with him to the Casco Street church, with the result that both he and his friends were converted.

Miller's meetings in Portland are of special interest to Seventh-day Adventists, for among those who attended the lectures was the Harmon family, who immediately took their stand with others eagerly awaiting their Lord's soon return. Of all the Harmon family, none listened more closely than 13-year-old Ellen.

The meetings in Portland were well attended, and the Christian church on Casco Street, where they were held, was usually crowded. Meetings were conducted during the day, as well as in the evening.

Miller's lectures attracted not only the city dwellers but many from the outlying areas. Some brought their lunches, picnic style, and made an entire day of it, coming for the morning meeting and staying until the end of the last meeting in the evening. However, there was nothing of the carnival

---

6   Ibid., 156.

spirit, no air of hilarity. With great solemnity the audience listened as in meeting after meeting Miller outlined Bible prophecies with an exactness that brought conviction to many hearts.

Like most people of that time, Ellen and her parents had believed that Christ would come only after the millennium, during which the world would be converted. But as they listened to Miller present a different idea, backed up by Biblical evidence in lecture after lecture, they became convinced that Christ was going to come in 1843, only a short three years away.

Like her parents, Ellen was a member of the Methodist Church. With other members of her family she accepted the teaching of the Second Advent during Miller's meetings in Portland in 1840.

Miller left Portland on the last Tuesday in March. Traveling by railroad and stage, he arrived at his home in Low Hampton on Friday night. He had been away from home nearly six months and had delivered three hundred and twenty-seven lectures.

Traveling with Miller on the stage en route home was a young minister who knew the keeper of the inn at a certain place where they stopped. The minister and the innkeeper were soon engaged in a conversation about Miller, which he could not help overhearing. The innkeeper asked the minister whether he had read the copy of Miller's *Lectures*, which had been lent to him several days before. The minister replied that he had read the introduction, and finding that Miller was not a "learned man," he had decided not to read further. This struck Miller as a good example of the way many people permit those who are supposedly educated to do their thinking for them.

During the month of May, Miller gave his first series of lectures in New York City. He then returned home, where he stayed four weeks. He was beginning to feel the pressure of the many details that constantly demanded his attention. But Miller's was no longer a lone voice in the proclamation of the Second Advent; others were now preaching the doctrine.

While there had been a limited exchange of ideas through the columns of the several Adventist papers that were being published, there had been no organized attempt to coordinate the efforts of the different groups, or to unify their thinking. Prior to 1840 there had not been much reason for unification, for Miller had been almost the only voice. But with the addition of other voices and with the rapid growth of the movement, the need of coordination became apparent. For this reason the Adventists, headed by Miller, Himes, Litch, and others, planned a general conference to convene in the Chardon Street Chapel, Boston, on October 14, 1840. This was the first of several such conferences that were held during the next decade.

Miller left his home on October 8 expecting to attend the conference. But he had traveled only as far as Fairhaven—a distance of about two miles—when he became ill with typhoid fever, a common sickness in those days, and was taken back to his home. His plans to attend the conference were thus frustrated. He had to be content with dictating a short message to the delegates a week later. In his letter he expressed keen disappointment at being "deprived of meeting those congenial minds in this good, this glorious cause of light and truth"; but he acknowledged that ". . . God is right; his providence is right; his ways are just and true; and I am foolish to murmur or complain. I have great blessings yet, more than I can number. I was not taken sick far from home. I am in the bosom of my family."

The conference convened according to plan. Among its leaders were Joshua V. Himes, Josiah Litch, Henry Dana Ward, Henry Jones, and Joseph Bates. The official printed proceedings fills almost two hundred pages and consists mainly of prepared addresses that were read at the conference. The expense of publishing the report was paid by funds that were raised largely by Joshua Himes.

With his health restored a few weeks after the conference, Miller lectured in Fort Ann from December 26 to 30. This series of meetings brought to a close his work for 1840.

CHAPTER 7
1840–1843
METHODS AND MEANS

Miller's first series of lectures in 1841 was held in the city of Boston. Beginning on January 31, it was the fourth such series to be presented in that city. Following this, he accepted the invitation of the pastor of the Baptist church of Andover, Massachusetts, to hold meetings in that city from February 21 to March 2.

About the fourth day of the Andover series, Miller received a letter, signed "Anonymous," containing a long list of passages from both the Old and the New Testaments. It was obvious that the verses had been quoted from memory without citing the references. The writer was evidently sure that the material proved Miller's views on the Second Advent to be wrong. The texts were followed by a single question addressed to Miller.

The next evening, before he began his formal presentation, Miller took the letter from his pocket and asked whether there was any person in the audience by the name of Anonymous; and if so, would he please stand up? He paused while the audience waited in silence for such a person to stand, but of course no one accepted the invitation. Then Miller read the "quotations" from the letter—which were actually misquotations. After he read each verse in the letter he read the correct version from the Bible, so that the audience would be satisfied that not one text had been quoted correctly. When he had finished, Miller asked again whether "Anonymous" would stand; but there was no response. Of course he had not expected any. Then he read the question at the bottom of the letter: "Mr. Miller, how dare you assert your theory with so much confidence without a knowledge of the Hebrew and Greek languages?" After a moment's pause, Miller replied, "If I am not acquainted with the Hebrew and

Greek, I know enough to quote the *English* texts of Scripture rightly." And with that, he launched into the evening's subject. "Anonymous" was never heard from again!

At times, Miller operated on a very tight schedule, with no time for rest. It was not unusual for him to begin one series of lectures the day following the conclusion of the previous series. So it was that having concluded the series in Andover on March 2, he began his fifth series in Marlboro Chapel, Boston, on March 3. From the conclusion of these meetings until the middle of April he lectured in Providence, Rhode Island, and Lowell, Massachusetts. Then, after an absence of about three months, he returned home for a well-deserved rest. At that time he estimated that since the first of October, 1839, he had traveled 4,560 miles and had given 627 lectures, averaging one and one-half hours in length, resulting in approximately 5,000 conversions. All things considered, this was no small accomplishment for a man who at first had said, "I can't go, Lord."

During the latter part of May, Miller held meetings in Addison, Vermont. Before the series ended he was suffering from a painful inflammation in his left leg, which forced him to return to his home. That he did so was fortunate, because the right leg also became affected. His condition did not begin to improve until the middle of June. It was fall before he could resume his lectures. This enforced rest was one of the few "vacations" Miller took during his public career.

This illness prevented his attending the second general conference, which met at Lowell, Massachusetts, June 15, 1841. Approximately 200 delegates were present. Considering the methods of travel and the distance and expense involved, this attendance was nothing less than remarkable. The conference reaffirmed its conviction that the day of the Lord was near, and adopted a platform of nine specific suggestions as to how the believers might more efficiently carry this truth to the world. These ranged from recommending "the practice of questioning your minister on the subject" to "the circulation of books" and "the establishment of Second Advent Libraries" in as many communities as possible. Almost from its inception, the Millerite movement made wide use of printed material, whether as broadsides, papers, pamphlets, or books.

About this time Himes introduced what was possibly the forerunner of our Easter and Christmas seals. In those days, letters were not placed in envelopes to be mailed, but the letter itself was simply folded into the approximate size of today's envelopes and sealed with a few drops of wax or a sticker. Himes came out with a sticker about two thirds the size of our present postage stamps, upon which was printed a Bible text or some sentiment relative to the Second Advent. This was the genius of Himes at work to make known the truth to as many people as possible. For that purpose he had joined with Miller, and to that purpose he directed all his efforts.

The third session of the general conference was held in Portland, Maine, October 12-14, 1841. Again, Miller was unable to attend because of speaking commitments. But he addressed to the conference a letter in which he urged the formation of a committee to examine, advise, and recommend those persons who might desire to lecture on the subject of the Second Advent in the name of Millerism. Such a committee would only recommend, for since Millerism was a movement and not a legally formed church body, it lacked disciplinary powers. But this attempt to maintain some degree of unity within the movement was a wise move, and indicated Miller's foresight.

The fourth session of the general conference, held in New York City late in October, was also unattended by Miller. The fifth was held in Low Hampton, Miller's home town, November 2-5. Perhaps the reason for holding it there was to assure Miller's attendance.

One of the important items of business at the session was the passing of a resolution naming certain persons as being "entitled to the confidence, prayers, and cooperation" of all the believers. Evidently this was a way of getting into the official records the names of those who might be recognized as speaking for the movement. Among those named were Miller, Himes, Litch, Jones, and Ward.

The sixth general conference session convened November 30 at the Chardon Street Chapel in Boston. At this conference an appeal was made for funds to further the publication and distribution of adventist literature. In response, almost $1,000 was raised. This would not be a large amount by today's standard, but measured by the daily wage of fifty cents to a dollar of that time, it takes on greater proportions. And the figure grows more impressive when we realize that this was neither the first nor last such offering to be taken.

The day before the convening of the sixth conference Miller began his sixth series in Boston. He spoke to large audiences through to December 9. It is probable that his lectures were incorporated into the general conference session, since the two meetings—the conference session and Miller's lectures—were held concurrently in the same place. Meetings in Dover, New Hampshire, from December 11 through December 19 concluded his work of 1841.

The first part of 1842 found Miller lecturing in Sandy Hills, New York. The final lecture in the series was delivered in the courthouse. At the close, a prominent lawyer, H. B. Northop, arose and, after gaining permission to speak, said he had come to the meetings with the specific purpose of finding flaws in Miller's arguments. He said he had listened to every word and every sentence with that purpose in mind, but that he could find no weakness in Miller's reasoning. He stated that after studying both sacred and secular history along with the prophecies, he had never heard any other theory that could compare with Miller's for strength of evidence. This voluntary testimony, coming from a locally well-known lawyer, made a favorable impression upon many in the audience.

During the 1830's and 1840's the pseudo-science of phrenology enjoyed great popularity. Phrenology was based upon the belief that a person's character could be interpreted from the shape and contours of his head. This belief was the result of the rapid progress made in the study of anatomy and physiology in the early 1800's, when popular belief ran ahead of scientific fact. It was believed, for example, that a certain "bump" or protrusion on the skull might indicate musical ability, while other protrusions might show that the person had a propensity for thievery. Scientific knowledge later disproved the value of phrenology, but in the mid-1800's many people had great confidence in it, and practitioners of the so-called science were numerous.

Early in March, 1842, Miller was lecturing in Medford, Massachusetts. During his stay there a mutual friend took him to visit a phrenologist. The phrenologist had never met Miller before, although like most people he had heard of him and knew of his work. But he was not sympathetic with Miller's message. Unaware of the identity of his subject, he began his analysis by commenting that the person had a large and well-balanced brain. While he was examining the bumps that supposedly indicated moral and intellectual powers, he said to Miller and his friend, "I tell you, Mr. Miller would not easily make a convert of this man to his hare-brained theory. He has too much sense!"

He continued his examination, unknowingly comparing Miller's actual head to Miller's head as he imagined it to be.

"How I would like to examine Mr. Miller's head," he said. "I would really give it a squeeze."

Putting his hand on the supposed bump of "marvelousness," he said, "There! I'll bet you anything that old Miller has got a bump there on his head as big as my fist." And he doubled up his fist to emphasize his point.

In the meantime, Miller and his friend were laughing heartily, enjoying the entire situation. But the phrenologist supposed they were laughing at his witty remarks, which only inspired more witticisms.

The man finally completed his examination in a more serious vein, but pronounced the head of his subject to be just the opposite in every way from what he supposed Miller's head to be. When he had completed his analysis, he began to make out his "chart" or report, according to the usual custom. And then, in order to complete the information, he asked for the subject's name.

Miller replied that his name was really of no importance, but the phrenologist insisted. "Very well," Miller replied, "you may call me Miller, if you must have a name."

"Miller...Miller"; the phrenologist repeated the name slowly as he wrote it on the chart. "And what is the first name?"

"They call me *William* Miller."

"What! The gentleman who is lecturing on the prophecies?"

"Yes, the same."

The phrenologist, very embarrassed, sat down without saying another word as Miller and his friend took their hats and left.

The *Signs of the Times*, which had come out in 1840 as a semi-monthly, became a weekly in 1842. It was only one of many Adventist publications, but the fact that the number of issues was doubled in two years gives evidence of its success, and of the importance of the printed page in the Millerite movement. Himes, who still published the Signs, was also adding new volumes to the Second Advent Library.

The city hall of Hartford, Connecticut, was the scene of Miller's series presented from March 22 to 28. At the conclusion of the meetings the Hartford *Christian Secretary* made the following observation: "One fact connected with this conference struck us somewhat forcibly; and that was, the immense crowd which attended the whole course of lectures. Of one thing we are satisfied, and that is this: unless the clergy, generally, present a better theory than the one offered by Mr. Miller, the doctrine will prevail to a very general extent."[1]

The point was well made. The clergy did not present a "better theory," and Miller's teaching did prevail to a great extent and exerted a larger influence than many had anticipated.

After returning home for a short period of rest Miller began another series of meetings in New York City. There he had an unusual experience. His name and reputation were such at this time that the mere announcement of his lectures usually assured him of a large crowd. Accordingly, Himes had arranged for the use of the Apollo Hall, a large and expensive building on Broadway. But the attendance during the first part of the series was disappointingly small. Some reasons for this were that the large city offered many

1   *A Brief History of William Miller*, 169.

competing attractions, and the people of the metropolis were sophisticated and blasé. But most serious of all, bad press reports had created a prejudice in New York. Litch records that Adventists had been pictured in the New York press as nothing less than monsters, "almost anything but civilized beings." And the Adventists had almost no friends in New York City. As a result, no one invited Miller or Himes into their homes as they usually did in other places. And because of their limited budget they felt they could not afford a hotel room. So they slept, at first at least, on the floor of a small anteroom just off the hall.

However, the situation improved as the meetings progressed. Those who did attend began to spread the word, and before the series ended on the tenth of May, the hall was full.

Another session of the general conference convened in Boston on May 24, 1842, with Joseph Bates as the presiding officer. This session proved to be of particular importance, for several reasons. Two of the resolutions that were adopted show that the delegates were deeply conscious of the shortness of time.

> *Resolved*, that in the opinion of this conference, there are most serious and important reasons for believing that God has revealed the time of the end of the world, and that that time is 1843.[2]

The second resolution logically followed:

> *Resolved*, that we should keep it distinctly in mind, that we are this year to do our last praying, and make our last efforts, and shed our last tears for a perishing world.[3]

Possibly the event of greatest importance to take place at this conference was not the adoption of a resolution, but the introduction of what proved to be a valuable and unusual aid in teaching the truths of Bible prophecy. For it was at this session of the conference that Charles Fitch and Apollos Hale introduced what they called a "chart."

---

2   Nichol, *The Midnight Cry*, 101.
3   Ibid., 102.

Early in the conference, Fitch and Hale produced a strip of cloth upon which they had painted the symbols of Daniel and Revelation. Fitch explained that he had been turning over in his mind for some time the idea that if something of this nature could be used, it would simplify the subject and make it easier to present important prophetic truths to the people. The delegates at the conference saw in the chart a fulfillment of Habakkak's admonition to "write the vision, and make it plain upon tables, that he may run that readeth it" (Hab. 2:2).

So impressed was the conference with the chart that it unanimously voted to have three hundred of them lithographed immediately.

Joshua Himes, James White, and many other early Adventist preachers later made good use of this chart to clarify their messages. In the absence of more sophisticated visual aids such as we have today, this simple chart made a valuable contribution to a better understanding of the prophetic symbols, so vital to Adventist truth.

Still another resolution of importance came from this session of the conference. For some time Adventists had observed the effectiveness of camp meetings in bringing about revival and reformation in the lives of their Methodist friends and others. If Methodists could use camp meetings so effectively, why could not Adventists? In fact, they reasoned that they would be criminally negligent if they did not. Consequently, the conference passed a formal resolution that in view of the shortness of time remaining to warn the world, a series of camp meetings should be held.

In this one general conference session we can see several of the important elements that made the Millerite movement the influence it was. Those involved shared a compelling belief in the nearness of Christ's return. While not all Adventists were willing to accept 1843 or any other specific year as the precise time, they all believed that His coming and the first resurrection were the next great events of prophetic history. Believing this, they were motivated by an overpowering burden to warn the "perishing world." They felt a very real and personal responsibility for those who had not heard their message and were therefore not prepared to meet the Saviour when He should come. Finally, the extensive use of printed matter, which characterized the movement almost from its beginning, the ready acceptance of Fitch's innovative chart, and the enthusiasm with which they moved into the camp meeting program—all illustrate the eagerness with which the Millerites adopted any legitimate means to spread their message. Failure to do otherwise, they felt, was to be "criminally negligent." There was about the Millerite movement in the days just preceding 1844 a freshness and vitality that appealed to the imagination, intrigued the mind, and captivated the heart. Is it any wonder that under the ministry of the Holy Spirit thousands embraced the message?

The Millerites demonstrated their sense of urgency and their efficiency by beginning their first camp meeting on June 28, 1842—just one month after the general conference—at East Kingston, New Hampshire.[4]

Twenty-six large tents were pitched and partitioned into family units. Most campers returned to their homes each night, as there were provisions for only a comparatively few to stay on the grounds. For those who arranged to stay overnight, a fee of two dollars per week covered the cost of "board and lodging in tents." It was recommended that churches and groups get together and provide for their own needs. The railroad granted special rates of 90 cents from Boston or Lowell, a distance of about 40 miles. Even at that, the fare was the equivalent of a day's wages. No doubt the leaders were themselves surprised at the response to their invitation to "come and participate with us in this great feast of tabernacles." For people came by every available means of travel, by horseback, by horse and buggy, by stage, and by train, until they numbered in the thousands. Reports in the papers estimated attendance from 7,000 to 15,000.

In many ways this camp meeting was not too different from those of today. Meetings were scheduled at regular

---

4 Individual groups of Adventists had held camp meetings prior to this. But the East Kingston camp meeting was the first to be authorized by action of the general conference, and is generally considered the first Millerite camp meeting. See Nichol, *op. cit.*, 111, footnote.

intervals throughout the day and evening, and the schedule was posted for all to see. Every effort was made to maintain proper order and decorum. Each group of tents was under the supervision of a tentmaster. Lights were kept burning throughout the night. There were several speakers, but Miller gave the only regular series of sermons. Others spoke only occasionally or on special topics. There was one minor difference—the men and women were seated on separate sides of the main tent.

John Greenleaf Whittier, American poet and man of letters, spent a short time at the campground. In relating the incident he told of seeing the two broad sheets of canvas upon which was drawn the figure of a man with its head of gold, the breast and arms of silver, the belly of brass, the legs of iron, and the feet of clay. To Whittier, the beasts, the dragon, and scarlet woman depicted on the other side seemed to be "oriental types and figures and mystic symbols translated into staring Yankee realities."

Such was the East Kingston camp meeting from which radiated an influence beyond human computation. So favorably impressed were the leaders with its benefits that before it ended they were making plans for others, and envisioned similar meetings being held all over the country, especially in New England, where the Millerites were most centralized.

The enthusiasm with which the believers accepted the camp meeting idea is indicated by the fact that 31 of them were held during four months of the summer and fall of 1842. Forty camp meetings were held during 1843, and 54 in 1844. Altogether the Millerites conducted 125 camp meetings, attended by an estimated half million people.[5]

Another far-reaching influence of the East Kingston camp meeting must be noted here. One of those who attended the meetings was Robert Winter, a visitor to America from England. He was converted to Millerism at the camp meeting and returned to England determined to spread the good news there.

The Advent message had been preached in England as early as 1826, five years before Miller began his public work in

5   Clark, *1844*, vol. 1, 39.

America. But the Advent movement did not take so definite a form in England as it did here, and less emphasis was placed on an exact time of the Advent. Nevertheless, the truth of Christ's coming was proclaimed. And when Winter returned to England in 1842 his message gave added emphasis to the truth that was already being preached. Many united with him in his work, and the judgment message was proclaimed in various parts of England.

In this way the influence of the East Kingston camp meeting reached across the Atlantic to touch the lives of our English cousins.

But the end was not yet. If a tent could be used for our own meetings, the Millerites reasoned, why could one not be used to reach the public? It could be utilized to hold lectures in the large cities where it was becoming increasingly difficult to secure the use of a hall. And it could be moved from city to city with little loss of time. The more they thought about the idea, the more enthusiastic they became.

Putting thought into action, the leaders presented the idea to the laymen. The size of a tent needed would cost money, lots of money. But scarcity of money has seldom hindered God's people when they were fired with a zeal to do His work. And zeal is one commodity the Millerites had in generous amount. Enthusiasm for the project spread, and when an offering was taken a little later it amounted to $1,000, the equivalent of several times that amount today. The purchase of the tent was thus assured, and an order was placed immediately.

The "great tent," as it was called, was first used in August at Concord, New Hampshire. Few people had seen one so large. It was 120 feet in diameter and almost 50 feet high in the center. With a seating capacity of 3,000 to 4,000, its very size was a novelty and therefore an attraction to the public.

The speed and efficiency with which the Millerites moved the tent from city to city illustrates the urgency they attached to their message. For example, the meeting at Concord ended about four o'clock on Monday afternoon, August 8. By Wednesday morning, August 10, the tent was pitched in

Albany, New York, where again thousands turned out and it was filled to capacity.

But we must return to William Miller and his experiences after the East Kingston camp meeting, which closed July 5, 1842.

About a week after the camp meeting, he went to Albany, New York, where he gave one evening lecture before taking a canal boat for Granville, where he held meetings from July 18 to September 23. Never one to miss an opportunity to speak on his favorite topic, he gave a lecture to fellow passengers on the boat. We can imagine him hanging up his chart and speaking to those who gathered around, curious to learn the meaning of the strange symbols pictured there.

On November 7 he joined Himes in holding meetings in the big tent at Newark, New Jersey. Then on the nineteenth they began a series in the Methodist church of New Haven, Connecticut. *The Fountain*, a temperance paper then published in New Haven, reported Miller to be "one of the most interesting lecturers we have any recollection of ever having heard," and one who "certainly evinces great candor and fairness in his manner of proving his points."

There were some among the Adventists who felt that Miller should be more definite in his statements regarding the time of the expected Advent. To them, Miller's time of "about the year 1843" was too general. In response to their demands Miller published a brief summary of his views regarding "the time."

These four statements stand out as most important:

> I believe God has revealed the time. (Isa. 44:7, 8; 14:20, 21; Dan. 12:10; Amos 3:7; 1 Thess. 5:4.)
>
> I believe many who are professors and preachers will never believe or know the time until it comes upon them. (Jer. 8:7; Matt. 24:50; Jer. 25:34–37.)
>
> I believe the wise, they who are to shine as the brightness of the firmament, Dan. 12:3, will understand the time. (Eccl. 8:5; Dan. 12:10; Matt. 24:43–45; 25:6–10; 1 Thess. 5:4; 1 Peter 1:9–13.)
>
> I believe the time can be known by all who desire to understand and to be ready for his coming. And I am fully convinced that some time between March 21st, 1843, and

March 21st, 1844, according to the Jewish mode of computation of time, Christ will come, and bring all his saints with him; and that then he will award every man as his works shall be. (Matt. 16:27; Rev. 22:12)[6]

Miller followed this statement by an article published January 1, 1843, entitled "Address to Believers in the Near Advent." In it he reaffirmed his belief that "this year, according to our faith, is the last year that Satan will reign in our earth." And he warned his followers that "this year will try our faith." Little did he realize just *how* severely their faith was to be tried before the year was out.

An example of the type of situation that began to plague Millerism took place in Washington, D.C. On Sunday, January 22, 1843, handbills and signs appeared all over the city announcing that "Miller, the-end-of-the-world man," would preach the next day from the steps of the Patent Office building. Shortly after noon the crowds began to gather until an audience estimated to number from 5,000 to 10,000 was present. All were quiet and orderly until someone stepped from the crowd and announced that there would be no speaker since, so far as it could be learned, Miller was not in the city. The person who made the announcement was never identified.

As the impact of the announcement registered, cries of "Boo!" "Hoax!" and "Humbug!" filled the air. In reporting the incident, the *Boston Mercantile Journal* credited "some printer's devil, or other mischievous boys" for the hoax. Printer's devil, mischievous boy—whoever it was, he plainly was no friend of Miller's.

The Millerite movement was now prominent enough to attract the attention of advertising copywriters, who are always on the lookout for a clever slogan or an eye-catching phrase. For several months there appeared a certain advertisement showing an angel flying in the heavens and carrying a banner inscribed "The time has come." This was an obvious take-off on the angel described in Revelation 14:6. The copy under the banner informed the reader that the time had come to enjoy the advertiser's product. Other

---

6   *A Brief History of William Miller*, 177–178.

advertisements used such phrases as "End of the World" or the "Second Advent" to catch the reader's eye, and then went on to suggest that the reader should use, for example, Smith's liniment "while time lasts."

During the first part of February, 1843, Miller lectured in Philadelphia, using the large auditorium of the Chinese Museum. The attendance was unusually good from the start, and continued to increase. On the evening of one of the last lectures the hall was packed with an overflow audience at an early hour. For the first half hour of Miller's lecture everything proceeded normally. Then a woman in the audience fainted, and when a door was opened to permit her to be taken out, part of the crowd waiting outside forced their way in before the door could be closed. At about that time someone foolishly shouted, "Fire," which of course caused pandemonium. Fortunately order was restored within a few minutes, and the meeting continued. But soon some outside attempted to force their way in. Under the circumstances, for the safety of everyone, the lecture was discontinued and the crowd dismissed.

The meeting held the next morning was also disrupted and those in charge, fearing for the safety of both the people and the building, ordered the meetings discontinued after the conclusion of that session.

CHAPTER 8
1843
HEADACHE AND HEARTACHE

People in the public eye, especially those who espouse unpopular causes, are frequently the target of erroneous statements, misquotations, and outright falsehood. And as the time approached when Miller believed the Advent would occur, he and his message became the object of sarcasm, ridicule, and verbal abuse.

Typical of this treatment was a New York *Herald* statement claiming Miller had decided upon April 3, 1843, as the date of Christ's coming. The truth is that Miller had carefully avoided citing any specific date for the Advent, believing that the Bible did not reveal that information. But the rather wide circulation of this false report caused a certain Prof. Moses Stuart to reply that regarding "the men of April 3rd, 1843, I would respectfully suggest, that in some way or other they have, in all probability, made a small mistake as to the exact day of the month when the grand catastrophe takes place—the first of April being evidently much more appropriate to their arrangements than any other day in the year." This, of course, was an obvious reference to April Fools' Day.

As remarks and articles of this nature came to Miller's attention in an increasing number, he thought it best to formulate a statement of his beliefs, which he did through the columns of the *Signs of the Times* in a letter dated February 4, 1844.

The reply was short and to the point. In it, Miller stated he believed that Christ would return "sometime between March 21st, 1843, and March 21st, 1844." He had not, he said, advocated any other time, nor had he specified any day within that time period. As to his personal life, he had a wife and eight children, all of whom shared his beliefs. He owned a small farm from which his family made its living. In regard to his finances, he stated that he had "no funds or debts." He had contributed more than $2,500 (a considerable sum in those days) of his own money to the cause. This had been supplemented to a small degree by gifts that God had given through the generosity of friends. As was Miller's custom when speaking through the *Signs*, he addressed the article to "Brother Himes," and he signed it simply "William Miller."

The small farm to which Miller referred had at one time consisted of some 170 acres, not all of which could be cultivated. It consisted of a 96-acre tract on the south side of a road and another 70 acres, divided into two parcels, on the north side. When Miller gave up farming to spend full time in lecturing, he "let out" his farm to one of his sons for $100 a year. He also sold him $500 worth of livestock. A little later he sold 70 acres to his son-in-law. Miller used this money to meet the expense of traveling and printing while he carried on his work. He was a "self-supporting" worker. Although he carried a license to preach, he was never ordained to the ministry and was never on the payroll of any church or religious body.

That Miller was subjected to almost unprecedented abuse by most of the secular press—and by much of the religious press, as well—is apparent to anyone who inspects the papers of his day. A certain amount of such abuse is part of the price to be paid for public prominence.

While almost no secular publication defended Miller's cause, there were a few whose editors took exception to the vulgar witticisms and ribaldry to which many papers resorted. Some sincerely felt that Miller's position deserved more serious treatment than its opponents were giving it. An article published in Miller's home county by the Sandy Hill *Herald* illustrates this attitude. It stated that although the paper did not subscribe to the doctrine taught by Miller, it felt that Miller was entitled to more serious treatment than being denounced as a "fanatic," "liar," and "deluded old fool." Speaking of Miller, the article stated that "we doubt not that he is sincere," and suggested that some of Miller's opponents should "take the pains to investigate" his teaching. In conclusion, the article stated that "if Mr. Miller is in error, it is possible to prove him so, but not by vulgar and blasphemous witticisms and ribaldry."

In much the same vein was an article that appeared in the Pittsburgh (Pennsylvania) *Gazette*, stating that the paper could see no reason for the reproach heaped upon Miller for propagating an honest opinion. The article strongly suggested that those who were denouncing Miller were only "whistling in the dark" to keep up their own courage.

At the close of his lectures in Philadelphia, where his meetings were closed prematurely as a safety measure, Miller went to Trenton, New Jersey. There, in response to the personal invitation of the mayor, he lectured for three days. The meetings were well attended. But the fact that Miller was in the city at the invitation of the mayor did not prevent the press from printing some unkind articles. The following is a case in point:

> Mr. Miller has been holding forth on his narrow-minded humbug at Trenton to large audiences....This Miller does not appear to be a knave, but simply a fool, or more properly a monomaniac. If the Almighty intended to give due notice of the world's destruction, He would not do it by sending a fat, illiterate old fellow to preach bad grammar and worse sense down in Jersey![1]

It is said of Noah that "the world made merry at the folly of the deluded old man." The same was true of William Miller. "Few men have been called to endure so great an amount of reproach as fell to his lot; and few could have endured it as he did. He was human, and shared in all the weaknesses common to humanity; but whenever he failed to endure the smart of undeserved wounds with all the sweetness of gospel charity, no one more sincerely regretted it than he did; and his liability to err in this respect was with him a subject of many prayers and tears."[2]

We who are living today can look back on Miller's treatment by the public press with the realization that Miller lived at the beginning of an era that was characterized by

---

1   Nichol, *The Midnight Cry*, 131.
2   James White, *Sketches of the Christian Life and Public Labors of William Miller* (Battle Creek, Michigan: Seventh-day Adventist Publishing Association, 1875), 217.

its robust reporting. There were few professional newspaper reporters as we know them today, and newspaper ethics were nonexistent. A publishing world that referred to Miller as a fool in 1844 also referred to Lincoln's Gettysburg Address as "the silly remarks of the President" in 1863. The Chicago *Times*, in reporting the ceremonies at the dedication of Gettysburg, made a statement to the effect that every American must be embarrassed as he reads the foolish words of the man who has to be pointed out as the President of the United States to intelligent foreigners. Some political cartoons pictured Lincoln as a baboon. Such was the price of fame.

Although Miller endured the abuse patiently, he longed for the time when it would come to an end. But it would end, he was sure, only with the advent of Christ. From a letter written to his friend Sylvester Bliss, on September 11, 1844, we catch a fleeting glimpse of his feelings:

> What then will be my feelings, when faith will end in sight, and hope in fruition?...No more a stranger in this giddy world,...no more to meet the scoffs of friends or foes, or meet the upturned lip, or curl of scorn from that black coat, and hear the oft-repeated epithet, in accents of deep derision, *"There goes old Miller."* My soul rejoices when I think a few more days, at most, and all these scenes will be forgotten in the eternal sunshine of his glory. Why not begin the song of everlasting gratitude to God for this blessed hope.[3]

After concluding his lectures in Trenton, Miller visited friends on Long Island, during which he was interviewed by the editor of the *Gazette and Advertiser*. In reporting the interview, the editor referred to Miller as having been the object of more abuse and ridicule than any other man then living.

The editor continued by stating that other editors had assured him that Miller was totally insane. But, quite to the contrary, he had found Miller able to discuss religious subjects with a coolness and soundness of judgment that caused him to say to himself, "If this be madness, then there is method in it."

---

3   Ibid., 291, 292.

Even so mild a compliment as this in the public press must have been to Miller like a cool breeze on a hot day.

The year 1843 was not one of Miller's best years. It had begun with the hoax in Washington, D.C., for which he was in no way responsible, but which did his cause no good. In February there were the disrupted meetings in Philadelphia. False rumors, abuse, and ridicule were increasing. Added to these problems, or possibly because of them, was a period of illness that sent him to his home for a time of enforced rest.

He suffered from a number of boils and carbuncles, which seemed to drain his system of its vitality. On the third of May, after his difficulty had begun to improve, he wrote, "My health is on the gain, as my folks would say. I have now *only* twenty-two boils, from the bigness of a grape to a walnut, on my shoulder, side, back and arms. I am truly afflicted like Job, and have about as many comforters, only they do not come to see me, as Job's did."[4]

Miller's health continued to be poor until the last part of May. He was confined to his bed much of the time, not only because of the boils but because of a fever. Not until the first of July was he able to walk around the house. But from then on he continued to improve. By the first part of September he was able to give a series of lectures in North Springfield, Vermont. The fall months were filled with lecturing in the New England area.

To the headache of ridicule from outside the movement was now added the heartache of fanaticism within the ranks. On the fall tour following his illness, Miller learned that some of those who had embraced the message of the Second Advent had become extreme in their beliefs and practices. In the opinion of some, any person who attached himself to the Millerite movement or who expressed any degree of sympathy with its teachings was, by that very circumstance, a "fanatic." But there are few groups, religious, social, or political, who do not attract those who by the very nature of their personalities become extreme in their application of the group's practices and principles. The Millerite movement was no exception. It has always been part of Satan's plan to use fanaticism to cloud true issues, to confuse minds, and

[4] *A Brief History of William Miller*, 214, 215.

to turn attention from truth to error in an attempt to defeat God's purposes. No reformation in the history of the church has been carried out without such obstacles.

To realize how easy—and perhaps even natural—it was for fanaticism to take root among the Millerites, we have only to recall that the movement was composed of persons from various denominations, with almost every conceivable spiritual background, and lack of background. Their one common denominator, the concept that gave them unity, was their belief in the near advent of Christ.

In the early days of their movement, Adventists had recognized the possibility of fanaticism rising among them. They had, in fact, adopted a plank to minimize this very danger as part of their platform at their first general conference, held in October, 1840.

Early in 1843 Miller had issued a strongly worded caution against the rise of fanaticism, and had suggested a remedy: searching the Word of God for truth.

But the best human effort could not prevent fanaticism from becoming a thorn in the flesh of the Millerite movement any more than in Paul's day, or in Luther's. We note two or three instances to help us understand some of the problems faced, and the way in which they were met.

There was the case of John Starkweather. Starkweather had accepted Miller's teaching in 1842. As a graduate of the Andover Theological Seminary he had previously been a minister in the Orthodox Congregational Church and a pastor in the Marlboro Chapel in Boston. At the time he accepted Miller's teachings, however, he was without a church. Since Himes was obliged to preach quite often in places other than Boston, Starkweather was called to serve as assistant pastor at the Chardon Street Chapel, where he assumed his new duties in October, 1842. Tall and pleasing in appearance, equipped with a powerful but pleasant voice, and with a reputation for superior sanctity, he had no difficulty in filling the chapel in which he held meetings every night. His favorite topic was the necessity of preparing for the Saviour's coming, a subject that is appropriate at any time, but which was especially so when the Advent was expected in 1843.

However, Starkweather had some strange ideas about personal sanctification which he made not only a test of readiness for the Lord's coming but also a test of Christian fellowship. He taught that one's conversion, alone, no matter how genuine it might be, did not restore one to God's favor. In addition, there must be a "second work," which usually was accompanied by some physical manifestation. Temporary loss of physical strength and other cataleptic phenomena were especially regarded by Starkweather as evidence of God's power in the sanctification of those who were "sealed."

Starkweather's movement gained ground during the winter of 1842, while Himes was away from his church much of the time filling speaking appointments. When Himes returned in the spring of 1843 and learned what the situation was, he determined to stop the rising tide of fanaticism at once. Accordingly, he called a meeting of his church members in April with the purpose of taking a once-and-for-all stand on the issue. Hoping to avoid a direct confrontation of personalities, he calmly outlined to his congregation the history of various movements that had been destroyed, or whose influence had been minimized, by extremism. Then, without referring in any way to the present local situation, he exhorted his congregation to profit from the experience of others and thus avoid the rocks upon which the faith of many had been shipwrecked.

But Starkweather was not one to accept defeat without an open battle. Catching the purpose of Himes's remarks, he arose to speak. He became so vehement that Himes had no choice but to address the congregation again, this time bringing into the open the nature of the manifestations that had appeared among them, and pointing out in no uncertain way their disastrous results. Some of those who had regarded the manifestations as an evidence of God's power were so offended by Himes's remarks that they jumped to their feet to object; others literally ran from the room. Still others shouted that Himes was driving away the Holy Spirit by "throwing cold water" on God's work.

"Throwing cold water!" replied Himes. "I would throw on the whole Atlantic Ocean before I would be identified with such abominations as these, or suffer them in this place unrebuked."

At this Starkweather announced that "the saints" would thereafter meet in another place, and he and his followers walked out of the building. Thus Starkweather became the leader of a new party. He held separate meetings, and by extending his influence to other places, gained a number of followers. His teachings were not countenanced by Miller or by Miller's real supporters, but in much of the public mind Starkweather was henceforth identified with the Millerite movement.

Fanaticism took many forms just before and immediately after the disappointment of 1843–1844. One group placed a literal interpretation upon Christ's teaching that His followers must "become as little children." Consequently, they made it a part of their practice to creep like little children as an evidence of their humility. They crept in their homes, on the street, and, in some cases, in church. Another group taught that it was a sin to work. The leader of the group "worked" hard to win converts, walking great distances to broaden his base of influence. However, both he and his influence ended abruptly when he made a rope of his bedding and hanged himself. Each fanatical movement—and there were many—was used of Satan to divert attention from the real purpose of the Advent movement, and to some degree brought the true message into disrepute in the minds of many who had little or no understanding of the true situation.

Because of his illness during the spring and summer of 1843, Miller was for a time not fully aware of the fanatical divisions within the ranks of the movement. But on his tour into Massachusetts he became aware of the situation and lost no time in dealing with it. Through the columns of the Signs, by the spoken word, and with every means available, he sought to discourage extremism in all its manifestations, and to divorce the movement from all fanatical influences.

Elder James White, who knew William Miller personally, wrote,

> From personal acquaintance with Mr. Miller, and a thorough knowledge of his teachings, we are happy to

state that during his entire public life he had no sympathy whatever with those teachings and influences which lead to fanaticism.[5]

In his first letter to the *Signs of the Times* on fanaticism, Miller expressed his disappointment at the "wild and foolish extremes" of some of the professed believers. In regard to the working of miracles, he stated that he had "no faith in those who pretend beforehand that they can work miracles." He pointed out that "whenever God has seen fit to work miracles, the instruments have seemingly been unconscious of having the power, until the work was done." The result of fanaticism, he said, is "to draw off Adventists from the truth, and to lead men to depend on the feeling, exercise, and conceit of their own mind, more than on the word of God." He closed his letter with an appeal that they all might "follow on to know the Lord."[6]

It must be remembered that Miller was the leader of a movement, not the head of a legal body. He could not discipline; he could only suggest and recommend. So in spite of all that he and his associates could do, fanatical minorities continued to arise, divide, and distract. It is an unfortunate paradox that he who detested fanaticism has been for so long identified with that very thing in the minds of many people.

The Millerite movement was only one of several that clamored for attention in the mid-1800's. The questions of temperance and women's suffrage agitated the minds of many. But most explosive of all was that of abolition and slavery. We cannot dwell at length on these matters. But neither can we ignore them, for they were very much a part of the American scene in Miller's time and, as such, touched his life and influenced his thinking.

We have previously noted that Joshua V. Himes was for a time associated with William Lloyd Garrison, the abolitionist. It required genuine courage to be an abolitionist in those days, for the movement was not popular. In 1835 Garrison was dragged by a mob through the streets of Boston, and threatened with lynching. Most people, even in the North,

---

5 James White, op. cit., footnote on p. 249.
6 *A Brief History of William Miller*, pp. 222–224.

regarded abolitionists as dangerous, radical disturbers of the peace.

In the early years of his public work, Miller shared these sentiments. All of us reflect to some degree the thinking of our time and of the society in which we live, and Miller was no exception. He viewed abolition as a dangerous evil. He was never one to be halfhearted on any question, and he wrote about abolition with the same vigorous and colorful style that he used when he spoke of the Second Advent. In one letter he wrote about the "fire-skulled, visionary, fanatical, treasonable, suicidal, demoralizing, hot-headed set of abolitionists."

It is to Miller's credit that he did not allow himself to be sidetracked from his main purpose of preaching the Second Advent to become involved in the social issues of the day. It is also to his credit that he later came "to espouse the much-maligned abolitionist movement."[7]

In this connection the following letter is of interest. It was addressed to Miller on November 8, 1844, and for obvious reasons was sent to him by personal messenger.

> DEAR BROTHER MILLER: The bearer is a fugitive from the iron hand of slavery and, as appears from letters in his possession and his own statements, of some considerable consequence to his claimant. His master, with United States officers, is in hot pursuit of him. Not being acquainted with anyone in your section that would be more ready to feed the hungry and direct a stranger fleeing to a city of refuge than yourself, I have directed him to you.
>
> I think it is best for him to keep on through Vermont as far as Vergennes or Burlington, at least, before he strikes the Lake. You will probably be able to refer him to some abolitionist on his way north. Should you think any other course more safe, you will advise him.
>
> Yours for the slave,
(signed) PHILANDER BARBOUR
> If anything important transpires, let me know it.

---

7   Nichol, *op. cit.*, 260.

With this short detour into another side of Miller's personal life, and a brief glimpse of the underground railroad in action, we must return to our main theme.

CHAPTER 9
1843-1844
COME OUT OF HER, MY PEOPLE

As the expected time for the second coming of Christ approached, the Millerites began to ask themselves some very practical questions. Should they give up their trades and professions these last few months, and devote all their time in preparing themselves and others for the end? Would it be a denial of their faith to do otherwise?

An editorial in the *Signs of the Times*, February 22, 1843, entitled "Occupy Till I Come," discussed this question. It concluded that while certain individuals might be justified in giving their entire time to the cause, this should not be true of those who made up the movement in general.

> To conclude that we have nothing to do by way of laboring for the souls of others or providing for our temporal wants, and therefore spend our time in idleness is to disobey God and bring dishonor on the cause we have espoused. Let everyone therefore "be diligent in business, fervent in spirit serving the Lord." Let him visit the sick, feed the hungry, clothe the naked, administer to the afflicted, relieve the wants of the destitute, and do good as he may have opportunity.
>
> Let him also continue to sow his field and gather the fruits of the earth while seedtime and harvest may continue, neglecting none of the duties of this life. But watch, stand fast in the faith, lead holy lives, showing to the world that this is not our home, that our affections are not set on the things of this world.[1]

Sensible counsel, indeed. And in general, this advice was followed. There was a small number, however, who were impressed to lay aside their regular employment in order to devote their full time to proclaiming the Advent.

---

1 Nichol, *The Midnight Cry*, 132, 133.

The middle of December, 1843, found Miller lecturing in Lewiston, New York. There, as in several other places, he was challenged to public debate by a representative of the Universalists. But he refused to take part in such a debate, not, he said, because he was afraid, but because to do so would be considered an admission that his opponents *might* be right. This he was unwilling to concede. He justified his position by citing Christ's refusal to contend with the devil, and His words "The Lord rebuke thee, Satan!" "And," said Miller, "so say I to his ministers."

Early in 1843 the Millerites built a large tabernacle on Howard Street in Boston in order to accommodate the crowds that attended their lectures. A year later, in January, 1844, Miller gave a series of lectures in the Howard Street Tabernacle, as it was called. Although this was his seventh series in the city, the building was usually filled to its capacity of three thousand for his meetings. On February 7, 8, and 9 Miller lectured in New York City, and the audience was estimated at 5,000. Himes was fulfilling his promise to open the door to the larger cities of America.

However, it was becoming increasingly difficult for the Millerites to secure the use of Protestant churches in those cities. Ministers who had welcomed their message in the 1830's because it brought revival and increased their church membership, now resented the growth and influence of the movement. Friendship was largely replaced by resistance and in some cases by open hostility. In many places ministers began to preach against the Millerite message. The "Big Tent" served to good advantage in cities where halls and auditoriums could not be secured because of the growing hostility. The Howard Street Tabernacle made such a valuable contribution to the cause in Boston that soon others were built in Cincinnati, Akron, and Cleveland.

While Miller's message was attracting large crowds, and his followers were numbered in the thousands, his name was seldom seen in the religious press. On those rare occasions when reference was made to his work, it was almost always in a bad light. The first issue of the *Signs of the Times*, for example, carried an item calling attention to the fact that a certain "Rev. Parsons Cook of Lynn (Mass.) asserts in the *Puritan* that Mr. Miller's lectures are more demoralizing than the theater!" The *Signs* then called upon its readers either to verify or refute this charge, based on their own personal experience. "We should be pleased to hear from those societies with whom Mr. Miller has lectured. Will they tell us whether this charge is true? What has been the effect of Mr. Miller's labors among them? Brethren, please let us hear soon."

It is probable that some of the unfavorable statements that appeared in the press were made by people who had never attended any of Miller's lectures but who assumed that his converts were frightened into accepting his message by his vivid portrayal of the end-of-the-world scenes. There is no evidence, however, that Miller ever resorted to "scare" tactics, although his meetings were characterized by unusual solemnity.

Ellen G. White, who as a young girl attended two series of Miller's lectures, described the congregations as "unusually quiet and attentive." Although Miller was an interesting speaker, his method of delivery was not flowery. It was remarkable neither for its grace nor eloquence. He presented the message in a calm, factual manner, and supported his arguments with Biblical proof. But the convicting power of the Holy Spirit accompanied his words, with the result that many accepted his message as present truth for that time. The *Massachusetts Spy* of February 22, 1843, commented that Miller "has a good fund of historical and Biblical information, and a very retentive memory."

Jane Marsh Parker, the daughter of Joseph Marsh, a Millerite preacher, knew Miller when she was a child of eight. Fifty years later she recalled that Miller had a "strong mellow voice and earnest manner, making his most cultivated hearers to forget his homely phraseology and provincial pronunciation." Another contemporary described Miller's peculiar pronunciation rather oddly as "northern-antique."

In physical stature Miller was of medium height, and a little on the heavy side. His face was full and round, and his eyes, according to one observer, revealed "shrewdness and love." Even when he was in his sixties his hair was not gray, but a light glossy auburn. One noticeable characteristic was his shaking hands and head, the result of what was then called "a stroke of palsy." So severe was this affliction that it could be observed by most of those who made up his audiences.

It seems apparent that any influence Miller exerted on his audiences was not the result of a magnetic personality, an outstanding physical appearance, or an overwhelming eloquence. It was rather the result of the ministry of the Holy Spirit on the hearts of those who listened.

Most people knew of Miller only in connection with what the public considered religious fanaticism, and therefore they. formed opinions of him that were anything but complimentary. But Joshua Himes, who was associated with him for ten years, and who therefore probably knew him better than any other person outside his own family, considered him to be a man of more than ordinary mental power, an honest thinker, a humble and devout Christian, and a kind and affectionate friend.

By nature, Miller was a conservative and retiring individual. To impute to him the practice of frightening his audiences into repentance, with all the emotional display this would require, is to take him completely out of character. Although he preached in a day when it was customary for preachers to appeal to the emotions, Miller appealed primarily to the intellect through the reading of the Word of God. So conservative was he, in fact, that he was known to say when someone in the audience became a bit demonstrative, "I depreciate your loud 'Amen's' and `Praise God's.' "

Even Miller's best friends and most loyal supporters never painted anything other than a very modest picture of his platform ability. Miller himself never claimed to be anything other than a farmer who had a message and a conviction that God had asked him to share that message with the world.

It was probably this and the blessings of the Holy Spirit, that gave him the ability to hold the attention of audiences numbering in the thousands night after night. And he accomplished this without today's audio-visual aids and electronic amplifying systems.

There was about Miller that which enabled him not only to win thousands of laymen to his message but also to persuade a considerable number of ministers of various faiths to abandon certain of their former beliefs and cast their lot with his unpopular movement.

Perhaps one of the most remarkable things about Miller was his energy, his ability to keep going, to deliver as many consecutive extemporaneous addresses as he did, with so little rest. He was older than most Millerite preachers, but he set the pace for the younger men. In one ten-day period, for example, he gave 18 lectures at Lockport, New York, followed immediately by 17 at Buffalo in nine days. In 1843, when he was 61, he gave 82 lectures within the space of 47 days, with only five days when there was no meeting. He recorded that in the 12 years between 1832 and 1844 he delivered 3,200 lectures.

Miller's complete series consisted of 18 sermons, commonly called lectures, each from one to two hours in length. On many occasions, of course, he did not give the complete series. He frequently based the first lecture of each series on Titus 2:13: "Looking for that blessed hope, and the glorious appearing of the great God and our Saviour Jesus Christ." In Boston, he preached seven different sermons from this text.

Miller's strenuous schedule, with the endurance and the expenditure of physical and nervous energy it required, is evidence that he was blessed with a strong constitution. But in his later years, age and the strain of being almost constantly on the speaker's platform began to take their toll. There were times when his work was interrupted by illness. In fact, during his last years much of his work was done, not because he enjoyed good health, but in spite of poor health.

In the summer of 1836 he wrote to Hendryx of being confined to his home by what he called "a bilious complaint." In quaint language he related that he was "taken unwell while lecturing." But he added, "yet I finished my course of lectures." He was motivated by the fact that the building was "filled to overflowing for eight days in succession."

While Miller had more than ordinary intellectual strength, a thorough grasp of his subject, an overpowering conviction that his message was from God, and a sincerity that even his strongest opponents admitted, we must look in other directions for the reason for his success. One reason stands out above all others: *He was God's man, with God's message, on God's schedule.*

Thousands were led to embrace the truth preached by William Miller, and servants of God were raised up in the spirit and power of Elijah to proclaim the message. Like John, the forerunner of Jesus, those who preached this solemn message felt compelled to lay the ax at the root of the tree, and call upon men to bring forth fruits meet for repentance.[2] As John the Baptist heralded the first advent of Jesus and prepared the way for His coming, so William Miller and those who joined him proclaimed the second advent of the Son of God.[3] God called him to leave his farm, as He called Elisha to leave his oxen and the field of his labor to follow Elijah.[4]

God chose Miller to do a special work for Him, and commissioned angels to protect him, that his life might be spared until his work was finished. On some occasions Miller's message so enraged certain people that they planned to take his life as he left the auditorium. "But angels of God were sent to protect him, and they led him safely away from the angry mob. His work was not yet finished."[5]

It is much easier for us today to see God's hand in Miller's work than it was for the people of his time. Hindsight is always more perceptive than foresight. To most people of his day Miller was a religious fanatic; to some he was an object of ridicule; to others he was a man to be tolerated. Comparatively few recognized his message as coming from God. This should not surprise us, however, for it has always been so. The antediluvians listened to Noah's message for 120 years, but when the Flood came there were only eight

---

    2   Ellen G. White, *Early Writings* (Washington, D.C.: Review and Herald Publishing Association, 1945), 233.
    3   Ibid., 230.
    4   Ibid., 229.
    5   Ibid., 234.

people, members of Noah's own family, with enough faith in the message to act upon it. In John's day only a handful of people recognized the message that Christ was the "Lamb of God, which taketh away the sin of the world" as being God's message for them. So it was that while thousands were led to embrace the truth preached by William Miller, they were only a few compared to those who heard his message and rejected it as the product of an imaginative or unbalanced mind. The validity of a message cannot be determined by the number of people who accept it.

As the time of the expected Advent approached and the number of people accepting the message increased, many ministers and church leaders became jealously aware of the inroads Miller was making on their own congregations. Because of this, many of them began to take disciplinary action against those of their congregations who accepted the Advent doctrine. In addition to those who were disfellowshiped, many voluntarily withdrew their membership because they felt they were being denied their basic right of investigating the Scriptures to learn the truth for themselves, and of following it according to their consciences. In the summer of 1844 about 50,000 withdrew from the churches.

The attitude of the Methodist Maine Conference toward Millerism was somewhat typical of that taken by many churches during this period. Beginning about the time of Miller's second series of lectures in Portland, that church organization adopted a number of resolutions condemning the views of Millerism, and requiring its ministers to refrain from propagating them. Laymen who insisted on accepting and disseminating them were to be disfellowshiped.

The Harmon family passed through this experience. Ellen Harmon, it will be remembered, had attended both of Miller's series in Portland, Maine. With other members of her family she had accepted the Advent message as present truth and had, at her insistence, been baptized by immersion. In *Life Sketches* she related in detail how the pastor made a "special visit" to the family, and how, without inquiring as to the reasons for their belief or referring to a single text of Scripture, he advised them to quietly withdraw from the church and avoid the publicity of a trial. This they refused to do, preferring rather to have opportunity to defend their new faith. At the church trial the single charge preferred was that the Harmons had walked contrary to church rule. The next Sunday the presiding elder read off their names, seven in number, as disconnected from the church. He stated that they were not expelled on account of any wrong or immoral conduct, that they were of unblemished character and enviable reputation, but that they had been guilty of walking contrary to the rules of the Methodist Church. He also declared that a precedent had now been established and all who were guilty of a similar breach of the rules would be dealt with in like manner.

The practice of expelling those who accepted the teaching of the Second Advent naturally caused Miller great concern. As he had stated early in his public work, he had no thought but that his doctrine would be warmly accepted by the Christian churches, and it was never his intent to break away from them.

However, it was not the *use* of church discipline to which Miller objected, but its *abuse*. "The hypocrite uses it as a tool to make others think that he is very pious. The envious use it as a weapon to bring down those they imagine are getting above them. The bigot uses it to bring others to his faith; and the sectarian, to bring others to his creed, etc."[6]

In addition to expressing his concern privately regarding the practice of disfellowshiping those who accepted the Second Advent doctrine, Miller published a rather lengthy article in which he challenged the Protestant churches to give reason for their treatment of the Millerites.

What had the Millerites done, he asked, that they should receive such denunciation from the pulpit and in the press? For what reason were they being denied fellowship in the Protestant churches? The Millerite conclusions, he pointed out, had been formed deliberately and prayerfully, and were based on a sincere understanding of the Bible. Miller then called upon his readers to show from the Bible where his teaching was wrong. And until they were shown their error,

---

6   James White, *Life of William Miller*, 92.

he stated, they must continue to believe that Christ would come "in this Jewish year."

This appeal gave the churches an opportunity to respond to Millerism or to produce Biblical reasons for rejecting it. But there is no evidence that any attempt was made to respond to Miller's appeal. In general, the churches continued to reject the message of the Second Advent. With this rejection there began a spiritual decline among the Protestant churches of America. The spiritual apathy and steadily increasing conformity to worldly practices that accompanied the rejection resulted in a loss of power from which the churches have never fully recovered to this day.

Although the spiritual declension was noted by various church leaders, they were unaware of its cause and helpless to stay its progress. Ellen White attributes it to this turning against the message God had sent through Miller.

Until the spring of 1844 those who espoused Miller's cause were known simply as "Millerites." Although at first used in derision, it was a name that came quite naturally; it was a nickname, but a practical way to designate those who believe in the near coming of the Saviour as taught by Miller. But when it began to appear that the Millerites were going to be in this world longer than they had expected, they began to cast about for a name that would more properly describe them or their beliefs.

The editor of the *Advent Herald* stated that they had "no particular objection to being called 'Millerites'...but there are many of our number who do not believe with Mr. Miller in several important particulars. It is also his special wish that we should not be distinguished by that appellation." The editor then went on to suggest that the name Adventist might be an appropriate one, for it "marks the real ground of difference between us and the great body of our opponents." He pointed out that "the question of time...is not, nor has it ever been, the only, or the main question in dispute. In fact, there is a greater difference between us and our opposers on the *nature of the events predicted*, than upon the interpretation of the prophetic periods, or their termination."[7]

---

[7] Nichol, *The Midnight Cry*, p. 207.

From this it is seen that Millerism was based on more than a mere setting of time. Had this not been true, the entire movement would have evaporated following the second disappointment, if not the first. The focal point of Millerism was not the time of the advent, but its *nature*.

An important fact about Miller's teaching, but one that is often overlooked, is that none of the points that made Millerism unique—if taken one by one—was original with Miller. Miller's contribution was in putting them together, like a giant jigsaw puzzle, in such a way that they stood the test of Scripture. That these points did not originate in Miller's mind does not in any way minimize the importance of the ideas or of Miller's work. On the contrary, it was the fact that Millerism was *not* of human origin that made it supremely important. It was an angel of God, Ellen White tells us,[8] not human impulse, that moved upon Miller's heart to study the Bible. Unknown to him angels often opened his mind and guided his thinking to a correct understanding of Bible prophecy. He was led to find link after link until he had discovered in the Scripture "a perfect chain of truth."

Each of the main links of Miller's message was admitted by one or more of his opponents. But none of his opponents could agree with him or with one another on *all* points, for there was as much disagreement between his various opponents as there was between any of them and Miller. Therefore they could not disprove Miller's message without disproving the teachings of one another.

---

[8] Ellen G. White, *The Story of Redemption* (Washington, D.C.: Review and Herald Publishing Association, 1947), 356, 357.

CHAPTER 10
UNTO 2300 DAYS

As we have seen, Miller came to believe that Christ would come sometime between March 21, 1843, and March 21, 1844. His conclusion was based on his study of Daniel 8:14: "And he [the angel] said unto me [Daniel], Unto two thousand and three hundred days; then shall the sanctuary be cleansed." Without doubt this prophecy, which covers a longer period of time than any other, is one of the most significant of the entire Bible.

This prophecy, which began in Daniel's time, pointed forward "two thousand and three hundred days" into the future when the sanctuary would be "cleansed." To most Bible scholars, the time when the 2300 days would begin and end was shrouded in mystery. And since the book of Daniel was supposedly "sealed" from human understanding, few scholars made a serious attempt to unveil the mystery.

But Miller, convinced that the Bible is God's message to man, felt that it was intended to be understood by man. He believed that it is its own best expositor and that it would explain itself if studied with that principle in mind.

With these two ideas as his point of departure, Miller spent many hours over a period of two years making a detailed study of Daniel 8:14 and related texts.

Let us note here that the understanding Seventh-day Adventists of today have of the sanctuary is not the same as Miller understood it. Today we are clear, on the basis of the book of Hebrews, that the sanctuary of Daniel 8:14 is the heavenly. At one time, early in his study, Miller was of the opinion that the sanctuary represented the church on earth. After additional study he concluded that it was the earth itself. From this he decided that the cleansing of the sanctuary referred to in Daniel 8:14 and the cleansing of the earth by fire at Christ's coming are the same event. He then concluded that if one could determine when the cleansing of the sanctuary was to take place he would know when the Second Advent was to occur. So Miller set about to learn when "the sanctuary" would be "cleansed."

Let us briefly explore the development of Miller's belief that Christ was to come sometime between the spring of 1843 and the spring of 1844.

Basic to the interpretation of the 2300-day prophecy is the year-day principle; that is, the understanding that in prophecy a day represents a literal year, and that therefore the prophecy of 2300 days actually represents a period of 2300 years. The basis for the year-day principle is found in Ezekiel 4:6 and Numbers 14:34. These verses say, respectively, *"I have appointed thee each day for a year"*; and "After the number of days in which ye searched the land, even forty days, *each day for a year*, shall ye bear your iniquities, even forty years." We have already noted how Josiah Litch's prediction of the downfall of Turkey, based on the year-day principle, was fulfilled in 1840. In applying this principle, Miller and Litch were following a precedent established by able and mature Bible scholars before them. Augustine and the Venerable Bede and—among more modern scholars— Sir Isaac Newton used the year-day principle in interpreting Bible prophecy.

Moses Stuart, in his *Hints on the Interpretation of Prophecy*, pointed out that most of the Bible interpreters in the English and American world understood a day to represent a year. To such an extent was this true that although it was impossible to trace the origin of the practice, it had become an "almost universal custom."[1] It will be seen, then, that in using the year-day principle in his interpretation of Daniel 8:14, Miller was standing on firm ground. We have previously pointed out that other Bible students agreed with Miller on certain points. The use of the year-day principle was one of them.

Let us take a brief look at the manner in which the prophecy of Daniel 8:14 is interpreted to arrive at the year 1844. To do so we link it with chapter 9:24. In that verse another period

---

1 Uriah Smith, *The Prophecies of Daniel and the Revelation* (Washington, D.C.: Review and Herald Publishing Association, 1944), 204.

of 70 weeks (or 490 literal years) is introduced. This period, which is understood as beginning simultaneously with the 2300 day/year period, is divided into three shorter periods of seven weeks (49 years) sixty-two weeks (434 years) and one week (7 years). Miller believed, and Seventh-day Adventists believe, that both the longer period of 2300 days (or 2300 years) and the shorter period of 70 weeks (490 years) began at the same time.

According to Daniel 9:25, the event that was to mark the beginning of the two prophecies was "the going forth of the commandment to restore and to build Jerusalem." In order to understand the significance of this "command," or decree, we must remember that when this prophetic vision was given to Daniel, he was an exile in the land of Babylon.

The command, which was to mark the beginning of the prophecy, refers to a decree issued by a king of Persia—the Persians had captured Babylon—permitting the Hebrews to return to Judah, restore their civil state, and rebuild the city of Jerusalem.

Actually, there were three such decrees. But the first two were limited in their provisions and were preliminary to the third. The first decree was issued by Cyrus in 536 B.C., and is recorded in Ezra 1:1-4. The second was issued by Darius in 519 B.C., and is found in Ezra 6:1-12. The third decree, which really made effective the first two, was issued by Artaxerxes in 457 B.C., and is recorded in Ezra 7. That the decrees issued by these three kings are considered in their effect as one is indicated in Ezra 6:14, where the three are spoken of as "the commandment." It was the third decree, whose "going forth" was in the fall of 457 B.C., that marked the beginning of the 2300 days (years) and of the 70 weeks (490 years).

According to the prophecy, the 69 weeks (483 years), which composed the first two segments of the 70 weeks, were to extend "unto the Messiah the Prince" (Dan. 9:25). Beginning in 457, this period would end in A.D. 27. And it was in A.D. 27 after Christ was baptized, that He began His public ministry. "Jesus came into Galilee, preaching the gospel of the kingdom of God, and saying, *The time is fulfilled"* (Mark 1:14, 15). Jesus must have been referring to a specific time period that was fulfilled, and the only prophetic period that can be found to terminate then is the 69 weeks.

One short time period remains to be considered: the one week (7 years) during which the Messiah was to confirm the covenant and "cause the sacrifice and oblation to cease" (Dan. 9:27). This would be the last one of the seventy weeks, or the last seven years of the 490. By adding seven years to A.D. 27 we come to A.D. 34. Since this was the last of the seventy weeks, it marked the end of the period that was "determined upon thy [Daniel's] people," the Jews (verse 24). That year, A.D. 34, was marked by the stoning of Stephen, who thus became the first Christian martyr. By its stoning of Stephen, the Sanhedrin, the highest governing Jewish body allowed under the Roman government, confirmed its rejection of Christ and of the gospel. From that time the gospel was preached to the Gentiles to a greater degree than before, although the Jews as individuals were not excluded from it.

There is a final important detail to be noted about the 70-week prophecy. According to Daniel 9:27, the Messiah was to cause the sacrifice and oblation—that is, the sacrificial system—to cease, or come to an end, "in the midst of the week." Inasmuch as the 490-year period began in the autumn, as previously noted, the "midst," or middle, of a year starting from that season, would bring us to a spring. Consequently, the midst of the prophetic week under discussion, beginning in the autumn of A.D. 27, brings us, three and a half years later, to the spring of A.D. 31.

It was in the spring of A.D. 31 that Christ was crucified, thus putting an end to the meaning of the sacrificial system, since He Himself was the real Lamb to which the entire system pointed. And at the hour of Christ's death on the cross, God signified the end of the sacrificial system by tearing from top to bottom the curtain that separated the two rooms of the Temple that was the center of the system (Matt. 27:50, 51).

The seventy weeks account only for the first 490 years of the 2300-year prophecy, but they also provide the beginning date for the longer period.

Subtracting the 490 years from the 2300 years leaves 1810 years yet to be accounted for. We have already seen that the 490 years ended in the autumn of A.D. 34. When to this date we add the 1810 years remaining, we arrive at the autumn of 1844 as the terminal date for the entire 2300-year prophecy and therefore the year when, as Miller believed, Christ would come and cleanse the earth with fire.

Miller's method of calculation was simpler than that which we have outlined above, although he arrived at the same concluding date. He accepted the dates of Ussher in the margin of his Bible as the basis of his computation. Thus by subtracting 33 (Ussher's date of the crucifixion) from 490, he arrived at 457 B.C. (shown in the margin of Ezra 7) as the date of the decree to restore and rebuild Jerusalem. He then proceeded, as we have done, to subtract the terminal date of 490 years already accounted for from the total of 2300, getting 1844 as the terminal date of the longer prophetic period. Miller was not sure of the exact time of the year when the decree of Artaxerxes was issued, but he assumed that it was in the spring. For this reason, he selected the period between March 21, 1843, and March 21, 1844, as the time when the sanctuary would be cleansed.

Contrary to popular belief, Miller's distinctive and most important contribution to religious thought was not the setting of a time period within which he expected Christ to come, although it is this for which he is remembered. It was his teaching that Christ's coming would *precede* the millennium that was different. Before the rise of Millerism the common concept of the millennium was based largely on the writings of Daniel Whitby, who taught that the millennium was to be a thousand years of universal peace during which the world would be completely evangelized. According to Whitby, Christ's second coming would be at the *end* of the millennium. The position of the Millerites on this point is made clear in an official action taken by the Second Advent conference held in Boston in 1842: "*Resolved*, that we regard the notion of a millennium previous to the coming of Christ, when all the world shall be converted, and sinners in great multitudes saved, as a fearful delusion...."[2] It was, then, Miller's position as a premillennialist, that Christ would come *before* the millennium, as much as his date-setting that made him the object of ridicule.

It may be easy for people living today, who may not be acquainted with all the facts, to conclude that the Millerite movement was one big mistake, a blot on modern church history. This was not the case, for in the areas that made his teaching peculiar, Miller was wrong in only one major point, that of the event to take place at the end of the 2300 years. He was correct in his view of Christ's premillennial advent.

With respect to his interpretation and application of the prophetic symbols and time periods of Daniel and Revelation, Miller was correct with one exception. As we have already noted, he assumed that the commandment that marked the beginning of the 2300-day prophecy went into effect in the spring. In this he was mistaken. A later and closer check on the historical facts showed that it actually went into effect in the fall. But this error, from which God caused good to come, was later corrected. It will be noted that the error involved the season of the year, not the year itself. Speaking of the corrected date, Ellen G. White later wrote, "The computation of the prophetic periods on which that message was based, placing the close of the 2300 days in the autumn of 1844, stands without impeachment."[3]

We have noted that Miller's real mistake was in the event that was to occur at the end of the 2300 days. However, other Bible students have been mistaken about events connected with the coming of Christ, the end of the world, and other Bible teachings. George Bush, professor of Hebrew and Oriental literature at the New York University, was one of those who agreed with Miller on his chronology, but he wrote to Miller, "You have entirely mistaken *the nature of the events* which are to occur when those periods have expired." Actually, Professor Bush was just as mistaken as Miller,

---

2 Don F. Neufeld and Julia Neuffer, eds., *Seventh-day Adventist Bible Students' Source Book* (Washington, D.C.: Review and Herald Publishing Association, 1962), 659, Art. 1083.

3 Ellen G. White, *The Great Controversy*, 457.

for Bush believed that the great event prophesied was not physical conflagration, but moral regeneration.

The world has long ago forgotten Bush's error, but it seems reluctant to forget and forgive Miller for his. James White noted this inconsistency and, after calling attention to the rise of spiritualism, the increase in crime, and the spread of infidelity even in his day, said, "If this be the commencement of the temporal millennium, may the Lord save us from the balance." Then, after pointing out that both men were mistaken in the event to terminate the 2300 days, White asked, "And why should Mr. Miller be condemned for his mistake, and Mr. Bush be excused for his unscriptural conclusion? In the name of reason and justice we plead that, while the Christian world excuses Prof. Bush for his mistake, professedly pious men and women will not too severely censure Mr. Miller for his."[4]

---

4 James White, *Life of William Miller*, Introduction, 10.

CHAPTER 11
1844
MARCH 21—OCTOBER 22
DAYS OF GLORY

Miller did not spend time waiting for the expected Advent, which he believed would take place at least by March twenty-first of 1844. February found him lecturing as usual, this time in New York City. We shall never know what thoughts passed through his mind regarding what he was sure were to be his last sermons, for he left no record of his impressions.

Of one thing he was confident: he had done his best to fulfill the covenant he had made with God thirteen years before. Since then he had given 4,500 lectures, attended by at least a half million people. The Advent message was no longer "kept in a corner," as Himes had described it five years earlier.

For thirteen years Miller had told the world that it would soon hear its last sermon. For thirteen years he had warned as many as he could that soon would come that instant when time would cease to exist, and eternity would begin. That day had almost come.

Ellen G. White tells how the Millerites approached the hour of the expected Advent with a calm solemnity. Those who truly believed Christ was going to come had made a heart preparation for the event that brought them a sweet peace, a token of that peace that they expected to be theirs throughout all eternity. Their worldly cares were largely forgotten during the weeks immediately preceding the expected Advent, and they examined closely every thought and emotion as if it were to be their last.

According to Miller's reckoning, March 21, 1844, was the last day of the prophetic period within which Christ must come. At last the great day arrived! The Lord could come during the early-morning hours. But the sun crossed the meridian, the morning passed, and He did not come. Only the afternoon remained. It too passed. The evening came, and still the believers waited—waited and hoped and prayed. He must come before midnight! But, alas, midnight too passed. The next morning came, and still Christ had not come.

The bitterness—the galling bitterness—of that disappointment can be fully appreciated only by those who experienced it. To the disappointment of not being able to greet their Lord was added the ridiculing and scoffing of the unbelievers who now reveled in their seeming triumph. A few who had joined the movement because of fear now showed their true colors by uniting with the scoffers, saying that they had never really believed anyway. Others quietly deserted the movement and resumed their former manner of life, hoping to forget the entire experience. But a third group, the largest of all, was deeply disappointed and perplexed, but not discouraged. They did not give up their faith.

That the Millerite movement did not evaporate following this first disappointment can be attributed to two main factors. First, although everyone within the movement had agreed that the Advent was near, not all had agreed on a specific time for the event. Second, and more important, those within the movement were bound together by more than a date for the Advent. For this, as had been pointed out, was never the most important distinction of the Adventists. The ties that had originally bound them together in the Second Coming were now strengthened by the common experience of the disappointment. And most of them, having lost their membership in formal church organizations, had no spiritual home to which to turn. So, like live coals, they gathered warmth from one another. Also, they had in common, in spite of their disappointment, a deep faith in the Bible as the word of God. They also shared a conviction that if a mistake had been made it was they, not God, who had made it. And they believed that continued study and prayer would reveal any mistake they may have made.

Like others, Miller continued to look for the Saviour's coming, expecting it at any time. Four days after the disappointment he wrote to Himes that although the time had passed, he still expected "every moment" to see the Saviour descend from heaven. Only that hope, he said, gave him patience to endure the scoffs and taunts of the nonbelievers. He still believed that the Second Advent was "not far off."

During the days immediately following the disappointment Miller no doubt did a lot of self-examining. Had it all been a mistake? Was he, after all, a deluded old man, as people had often said he was? Could he live the past thirteen years over again, would he follow the same course?

In an article written on the second of May, Miller answered the last question by stating that if he were to live his life over again, in order "to be honest with God and man" he would have to do as he had done. He confessed what he presumed to be his error in computing the time, and acknowledged his disappointment. And he reaffirmed his belief that the day of the Lord was near, even at the door.

During the last week of May, the Adventists held their annual conference in the tabernacle in Boston. At one of the meetings Miller spoke for more than an hour, frankly confessing what he supposed was his error in computing the time at which the 2300 days terminated. He made it plain that he was not discouraged, nor was his faith in the Bible shaken. Although the supposed time had passed, it was evident that God's time had not passed. In conclusion, he referred his hearers to the message of Habakkuk 2:3, "For the vision is yet for an appointed time, but at the end it shall speak, and not lie: though it tarry, wait for it; because it will surely come, it will not tarry."

One who was present on that occasion and heard Miller's "confession" reported in the Boston Post of June 1 that he had never heard Miller when he was more eloquent or animated, or more happy in communicating his feeling to others.

As we mentioned previously, not everyone in the Millerite movement agreed with Miller on the specific time period within which the prophecy was to terminate. For several months prior to the disappointment of March 21, 1844, some had called attention to the tenth day of the seventh month of the Jewish calendar as the more probable date on which the prophetic period would end. In terms of our calendar, this date would fall on October 22, 1844. However, this idea was not accepted by Miller or by those who were most sympathetic with his cause, although Miller himself, a year and a half before the disappointment, had called attention to the importance of the tenth day of the seventh month in the Jewish economy.

A camp meeting was held by the Adventists at Exeter, New Hampshire, August 12 to 17. At one period during the third day of the meetings Joseph Bates, a prominent leader in the movement, was speaking. His message dragged a bit, and he found it difficult to put his heart into it, for, like others, he was puzzled and confused by the disappointment. While he was speaking a man rode up on a horse, dismounted, went into the tent, quietly greeted some friends and sat down by them. The rider was a Millerite minister, Samuel S. Snow; the friends were Elder and Mrs. John Couch.

Shortly after Snow entered the tent, Mrs. Couch arose unceremoniously and interrupted Bates. "It is too late, Brother Bates. It is too late to spend our time about these truths, with which we are familiar....Time is short. The Lord has servants here who have meat in due season for His household. Let them speak, and let the people hear them. 'Behold, the Bridegroom cometh, go ye out to meet Him.'"

Bates, perhaps hoping for a new explanation of the disappointment, was not offended by the interruption. "Come up, Brother Snow, and tell us," he invited.

After Snow had answered a few questions it was arranged for him to present his ideas in full the next morning. His sermon the next day was a powerful one. It was followed by an address on each of the remaining days of the camp meeting. Snow knew his subject well and spoke convincingly, so convincingly, in fact, that both Joseph Bates and James White accepted his message and left the camp meeting filled with enthusiasm for the "new light."

We have already noted that Miller's terminal year for the 2300-year period was March 21, 1843, to March 21, 1844. This was based on the assumption that the decree of Ezra 7, permitting the Jews to "restore and to build Jerusalem," went into effect at the beginning of 457 B.C. In terms of our calendar this would be in the spring. But additional study following the disappointment revealed that the decree had not gone into effect until near the *end* of 457. This would correspondingly carry the end of the prophetic period over to the autumn. Furthermore, Daniel 8:14 states that at the end of the 2300-day prophecy the sanctuary would be cleansed. This suggested some connection with the Day of Atonement of the Jewish economy, on which day the sanctuary was cleansed. The Day of Atonement, on the tenth day of the seventh month (Lev. 16:29, 30), corresponds to our October 22. Therefore, October 22, 1844, became the new date on which it was expected Christ would come.

This, in brief, was the "new light," preached by Snow at the Exeter camp meeting, that was accepted enthusiastically by Bates, White, and others.

Snow's idea was not the result of a sudden insight that had originated at the camp meeting. As early as February, 1844, he had published his views in the *Midnight Cry*, suggesting that the prophecy would not end until the *fall* of 1844. At that time, however, attention was being focused on March, and his idea received little attention. But at the camp meeting, after the disappointment, the mental climate had changed and the new concept was warmly received by many.

The period between March and October, 1844, was now viewed as the "tarrying time" of the parable of the ten virgins. It was time now, the Millerites saw, to give the "midnight cry" that Christ the Bridegroom was to come on October 22.

Not everyone received the new light with the enthusiasm of Bates and White. In fact, the editor of the *Advent Herald* reported that at first the definite time was generally opposed. In view of the recent disappointment this was quite understandable. Those who had formerly led in the cause were among the last to join in the movement. Among the most hesitant were Miller and Himes.

But the momentum of the "midnight cry" soon increased. In a short time the *Advent Herald* reported that the movement was sweeping over the land with the velocity of a tornado. It moved so rapidly, even reaching distant places, that it seemed not to be the work of men, but to spread in spite of men. It was a movement, the paper stated, that could be accounted for only on the supposition that it was the work of God.

Like a tidal wave the movement swept over the land. From city to city, from village to village, and into remote country places it went, until the waiting people of God were fully aroused. Fanaticism disappeared before this proclamation, like early frost before the rising sun. Believers saw their doubt and perplexity removed, and hope and courage animated their hearts. The work was free from those extremes which are ever manifested when there is human excitement without the controlling influence of the word and Spirit of God....Of all the great religious movements since the days of the apostles, none have been more free from human imperfection and the wiles of Satan than was that of the autumn of 1844....Farmers left their crops standing in the fields, mechanics laid down their tools, and with tears and rejoicing went out to give the warning.[1]

It was at this time, during the summer of 1844, that the voice of Millerism reached its greatest note of urgency.

When the Exeter camp meeting was in progress Miller and Himes were on a speaking tour that took them as far west as Ohio, so they did not hear the seventh-month-message presentation. They opposed it when they returned to the East. Up to the last of September Miller was hesitant about accepting the new date. But in the first week of October he expressed a change in his position, saying that though his attention had been called to the seventh month a year and a half before, he had not realized its full significance. He now saw a beauty, a harmony, and an agreement with the Scriptures that he had not seen before.

The enthusiasm with which the new message was being preached and received impressed Himes so favorably when he returned to the East that he could hold out no longer. In early October he too accepted the new date.

During the time between the Exeter camp meeting and October 22, the Adventists became the object of some of the wildest tales one can imagine. Many of the stories became so much a part of the history of the period that they could scarcely be distinguished from the truth; they became part

---

1 Ellen G. White, *The Great Controversy*, 400–402.

of the Miller legend. For one hundred years many historians and laymen accepted as truth tales, rumors, and reports that were based on hearsay and exaggeration. F. D. Nichol's scholarly and well-documented book, *The Midnight Cry*, published in 1944, has successfully refuted these tales and has to a large degree changed the attitude of many of today's historians toward the Millerite movement.

Events moved rapidly during the weeks and days just before October 22, 1844. As we have noted, leaders of the Millerites who had been slow to accept the new date eventually capitulated. Sylvester Bliss declared himself a believer in the seventh-month movement in the October 9 issue of the *Advent Herald*. Josiah Litch wrote on October 12 that he lived "in joyful expectation of seeing the King of kings within ten days." Charles Fitch, who was suffering from what was probably a bad case of pneumonia, also accepted the new date about the same time, but he did not live to experience the Disappointment, for he died on October 14. An effort was made during the last few weeks just before October 22 to scatter all the literature possible. The papers, *Midnight Cry* and *Advent Herald*, put out special issues. The editor of the *Midnight Cry* reported four steam presses going almost constantly to meet the need.

In preparation for the great event, the *Midnight Cry* introduced the idea of health reform. The October 19 issue, the last number before the anticipated Advent, carried this counsel: "Let us imitate Daniel, who would not defile himself with the king's meat....We can lay down no rule for others, but hope our readers will all keep the body under, as Paul did....Let us live every day on that food which is simplest, plainest, least exciting, and most easily prepared, and be very temperate."[2] Perhaps this was the first "health reform" message to be given by the Adventists. In any case, good counsel for twentieth-century Seventh-day Adventists.

With the exception of those who were called to preach, most of the Adventists continued their daily occupations. A few, as noted earlier, gave up their work in order to spend their time spreading the message. Some farmers were so sure the Lord was coming they did not plant their crops in

2 Ibid., 243.

the spring. Others did not reap their harvests in the fall for the same reason. But these cases were the exception. The counsel that appeared in the *Midnight Cry* was "Occupy till I come," but "let your actions preach in the clearest tones: 'The Lord is coming.'"

Restoration of stolen property and payment of debts became unusually common. A man who identified himself only as a believer in Millerism mailed five dollars in conscience money to the United States Treasury. Another man sent a larger sum to a New York insurance company with a note saying, "The Lord is at hand. This was unlawfully taken from you, and I ask forgiveness, for the Lord has forgiven me much." Even the editor of the *Midnight Cry*, to be sure that every obligation was taken care of, placed this notice above his signature: "If any human being has a just pecuniary claim against me, he is requested to inform me instantly." One newspaper reported that a believer brought an unpaid bill of $22.00 to a Millerite meeting and expressed concern because of his inability to meet the obligation before October 22. According to the newspaper account, sufficient money was quickly subscribed by others at the meeting so that the bill could be paid.

The last issue of the *Advent Herald* came out on Wednesday, October 16, 1844. On the front page was this statement: "As the date of the present number of the *Herald* is our last day of publication before the tenth day of the seventh month, we shall make no provision for issuing a paper for the week following....We feel called upon to suspend our labors and await the result."[3]

Miller had written, "I am almost home." This was the confident expectation of every sincere Adventist as the great day of the expected Advent dawned.

Early on the morning of October 22, 1844, most Millerites gathered in their churches to await the Advent. In communities where there were no church buildings the people met in the homes of various believers. Miller and Himes spent the day in the Miller home at Low Hampton. Many Adventists gathered in the large auditorium in Cincinnati. A firsthand account of the meeting appeared in the Cincinnati *Chronicle*. The report

3   Ibid.

estimated that there were 1,200 inside the building, with another 300 outside. The people were "very orderly," and there was "less excitement" than the reporter had expected. The minister (whose name was not given) preached what he said he was sure was to be his last warning to a sinful world. The meeting was closed before nine o'clock, and the people were advised to go to their homes, there to await the expected Advent that many felt would occur at midnight.

But midnight came and passed, and the Saviour failed to appear. What a bitter disappointment it was to the little flock whose faith had been so strong and whose hope had been so high.

Hiram Edson, about whom we shall hear more later, was one of those who experienced the Disappointment. He said, "Our fondest hopes and expectations were blasted, and such a spirit of weeping came over us as I never experienced before. It seemed that the loss of all earthly friends could have been no comparison. We wept, and wept, till the day dawn."[4]

Another Adventist, Washington Morse, described the experience in these words: "That day came and passed, and the darkness of another night closed in upon the world. But with that darkness came a pang of disappointment to the Advent believers that can find a parallel only in the sorrow of the disciples after the crucifixion of their Lord. The passing of the time was a bitter disappointment....And now, to turn again to the cares, perplexities, and dangers of life, in full view of jeering and reviling unbelievers who scoffed as never before, was a terrible trial of faith and patience."[5]

---

4   Ibid., 247.
5   Ibid., 248.

CHAPTER 12
1844
NEW LIGHT

At this point in the Miller story the questions arise: Why did God allow such a terrible trial of faith and patience to come to the "little flock"? Did He not care? Or had the Adventists been totally wrong in their understanding of the prophecies relative to the Disappointment? And if so, why did God allow the Disappointment?

The truth is, as we shall see, that God was guiding the movement all along. In retrospect we can see His hand as apparent in the Millerite movement as it was in His dealings with the first disciples at the time of Christ's first advent.

Perhaps we can better understand and appreciate the significance of the Millerite movement by noting some parallels between the experience of the Millerites and that of the disciples at the time of Christ. For this purpose, let us go back to Sunday of the Passion Week. On that day Christ rode triumphantly into Jerusalem as a king, "and a very great multitude" accompanied Him, shouting "Hosanna to the son of David" (Matt. 21:8, 9). Among those with Him were many who were the objects of His miracles: those whose eyesight He had restored, those whose ears He had opened. In that procession were those who could now walk only because He had given strength and vigor to their useless limbs; there were those who could now shout praises to His name only because He had loosed their tongues. And at the head of the procession, leading the donkey upon which Christ was seated, was Lazarus, whom Christ had raised from the dead.[1]

This was one of the two or three times in His entire earthly ministry when Christ purposely attracted attention to Himself. He had initiated the procession by instructing His disciples to go into the village and find an ass upon which He might

---

1   Ellen G. White, *The Desire of Ages* (Mountain View, California: Pacific Press Publishing Association, 1940), 572.

ride in the manner of royalty. Gathered in Jerusalem for the Passover were Jews from every land who would ask, "Who is this?" And back to their villages and cities and countries they would take the answer, "This is Jesus, the prophet of Nazareth of Galilee." The triumphal entry was part of God's plan to draw worldwide attention to the first advent, and the Scriptures point out that this entry into Jerusalem was a fulfillment of prophecy.

The parallel is apparent. God initiated the Millerite movement by placing upon Miller a burden he could not resist. In Heaven's schedule the time had come when worldwide attention must be focused on the time of judgment and the second advent of Christ just as the triumphal entry had focused attention on the sacrifice of Jesus and His first advent. The Millerite movement was instrumental in raising up the remnant church just as surely as the triumphal entry and connected events were instrumental in laying the groundwork for the formation of the Christian church.

The Millerite movement, then, was not a mistake. It was a definite part of God's plan. It was a fulfillment of prophecy just as surely as was the triumphal entry. "The first and second angels' messages were given at the right time and accomplished the work which God designed to accomplish by them."[2] "Miller and his associates fulfilled prophecy and gave a message which Inspiration had foretold should be given to the world, but which they could not have given had they fully understood the prophecies pointing out their disappointment."[3] "The preaching of a definite time for the judgment, in the giving of the first message, was ordered of God."[4]

As Jesus rode into Jerusalem that Sunday, how the hearts of His disciples thrilled! Soon, they were confident, He would proclaim Himself king, and they would become loyal subjects of His kingdom. Why else this kingly procession? But they did not correctly comprehend the purpose of Christ's earthly ministry. Blinded by tradition and worldly ambition, they expected Him to set up an earthly kingdom. How bitter, then,

---
2 Ellen G. White, *The Great Controversy*, 405.
3 Ibid.
4 Ibid., 457.

was their disappointment when, less than a week later, they laid His still form in the cold tomb.

There is a further parallel: "Like the first disciples, William Miller and his associates did not, themselves, fully comprehend the import of the message which they bore. Errors that had long been established in the church prevented them from arriving at a correct interpretation of an important point in the prophecy. Therefore, though they proclaimed the message which God had committed to them to be given to the world, yet through a misapprehension of its meaning, they suffered disappointment."[5] Speaking of the experience of the Millerites, Ellen White says, "The world laughed and mocked and reproached them; and those who believed without a doubt that Jesus would ere then have come to raise the dead, and change the living saints, and take the kingdom, to possess it forever, felt as did the disciples at the sepulchre of Christ."[6] "The disappointment of the first disciples well represents the disappointment of those who expected their Lord in 1844."[7]

But the parallel between the early disciples and the Millerites does not end here. God did not keep His disciples in disappointment long. For on the day the resurrection occurred, two of Christ's disciples walked to the village of Emmaus, about seven miles from Jerusalem. One of these was Cleopas, whose name is mentioned in the Bible only in connection with this event. The name of the other disciple is not given. The record tells how "Jesus himself drew near, and went with them. But their eyes were holden that they should not know him." Not recognizing their traveling companion, the two men talked with Him "concerning Jesus of Nazareth." Voicing their disappointment, they said, "But we trusted that it had been he which should have redeemed Israel." At this point, Jesus could have revealed His identity, but He did not choose to do so. Instead, He called attention to the prophecies concerning Himself. "And beginning at Moses and all the prophets, he expounded unto them in all the scriptures the

---
5 Ibid., 351, 352.
6 Ellen G. White, *Early Writings* (Washington, D.C.: Review and Herald, 1882), 240.
7 Ibid., 244.

things concerning himself" (Luke 24:27). It is doubtful that these prophecies were new or unknown to Cleopas and his companion, for the Jews were well versed in the Messianic prophecies. But, viewed in the light of the crucifixion that had so recently taken place, as their unknown Companion talked to them the prophecies took on a meaning that had not been seen or understood before. Cleopas and his friend began, plainly to see how the life and crucifixion of Jesus fulfilled prophecy. Admonitions, promises, and predictions that He had spoken to His followers took on added significance in the light of their new understanding.

Again, there is a marked parallel. God had compassion on the Adventists as He did on the first disciples. He did not keep them waiting long in disappointment.

Among the disappointed Adventists was Hiram Edson, a farmer, of Port Gibson, New York. Edson, with the other Adventists, was crushed at having his fondest expectation blasted. With others, he wondered whether it was possible that the rich Christian experience he had enjoyed while waiting for his Lord could possibly have been false. But he did not share in the doubts voiced by some of the other Adventists.

Very early in the morning of October 23, Edson, with several other men, went to Epson's barn. There, in privacy, they prayed earnestly to God, asking Him to give them strength to endure their disappointment, and, if possible, to give them light that would take away the discouragement of His people. For some time they wrestled with God as did Jacob. Finally, they were impressed that God would remove their perplexities.

Shortly afterward Edson suggested to a companion, apparently O. R. L. Crosier, a lay preacher, that they visit some other brethren to encourage them. The path they took was across a cornfield. Each of them occupied with his own thoughts, they walked silently. Suddenly, in the middle of the cornfield, Edson stopped. An overwhelming conviction had gripped him that instead of leaving the Most Holy Place of the heavenly sanctuary to come to this earth (another part of the sanctuary, as they understood it) on the tenth day of the seventh month, Christ had for the first time entered the Most Holy Place, where He had a work of cleansing the sanctuary to do before He could come back to this earth. Just as the Lord revealed His plan to the obscure Cleopas, so He revealed the reason for the disappointment to the little-known Hiram Edson.

As a result of Epson's enlightenment he, Crosier, and another Adventist, Dr. Franklin Hahn, secretary of the local county medical association, began to study the subject of the sanctuary more fully.

The result of this study, which took several months, was written out by Crosier and published in a special edition of the *Day-Star* on February 7, 1846. This paper was one of the more widely read Adventist publications after the Disappointment, and was published by Enoch Jacobs in Cincinnati, Ohio.

In his rather lengthy article, Crosier showed conclusively that the sanctuary to be cleansed is in heaven and is not the earth, as the Adventists had previously believed. The article, which also dwelt on the Atonement, the blotting out of sins not only in the sanctuary but in the lives of God's people, brought real encouragement to the disappointed believers. Not until about ten years later, in the 1850's, did further study reveal the "investigative judgment," a term coined by James White.

Stepping out by faith, Edson, Hahn, and Crosier ordered 2,000 copies of the *Day-Star* extra to be printed, at a cost of thirty dollars. The three men agreed to pay half the cost of printing, with the understanding that the other half would come from the sale of the publications. So limited were their financial resources that they had difficulty in raising their share of five dollars each. In fact, Edson sold some of his wife's silverware to pay for his share.

Copies of the *Day-Star* extra fell into the hands of Ellen Harmon, James White, and Joseph Bates. Ellen Harmon—she had not yet married James White—later wrote that God had showed her that Crosier's article contained true light on the cleansing of the sanctuary. She stated it was God's will that Crosier write the article, which she felt fully authorized by the Lord to recommend to "the saints."[8]

We note again, then, that the mistake made by the Adventists was not one of *time*, but of *event*. The cleansing of the heavenly sanctuary did begin on October 22, 1844; the investigative judgment did begin on that date.

In speaking of the first disappointment, Ellen White wrote that God's "hand covered a mistake in the reckoning of the prophetic periods. Those who were looking for their Lord did not discover this mistake, and the most learned men who opposed the time also failed to see it."[9] God had certain purposes, which in His wisdom He wanted to accomplish through the Millerite movement and the disappointments. Those purposes could not have been accomplished had they understood the prophecies correctly. Therefore God covered the mistake from their understanding very much as Christ made the eyes of Cleopas and his friend "holden that they should not know him" on the way to Emmaus (Luke 24:16).

We may never know on this earth all of God's purposes in permitting the disappointments of 1843–1844. But we do know that "the first and second angels' messages"—in connection with which the disappointments occurred—"were given at the right time and accomplished the work which God designed to accomplish by them."[10] Satan would prefer that God's people look to the future, to a "more convenient season," for the events connected with the judgment, the close of probation, and the coming of Christ. But by the preaching of a definite period within which the Advent was expected, they were made to look to the present for the necessary

---

8   Edson later issued an invitation to others who accepted the sanctuary truth to attend a conference, which was held in 1846. To this conference came Joseph Bates, who presented his newly found seventh-day-Sabbath truth. Just as Bates had received the sanctuary teaching from Edson, so Edson and Hahn now accepted the Sabbath truth from Bates.

It appears that with this exchange of ideas the Port Gibson group were the first Adventists to accept both the sanctuary and the Sabbath truth. However, Crosier refused to embrace the seventh-day Sabbath, and eventually he lost all contact with the Adventists.

9   Ibid., 235.

10   Ellen G. White, *The Great Controversy*, 405.

preparation. In this way, God designed to arouse His people and to bring them to a testing point.

A second important work was to be accomplished by the Millerite message. Having been brought to consider Christ's advent as imminent, God's people were brought to examine their hearts and to see their true condition of worldliness and backsliding. God, in this way, separated His people from the corrupting influences of the world.

There were those who had been motivated through fear to accept the Millerite message but who really did not love the appearing of Jesus. Their profession was a coat they had put on, but it did not affect the heart or purify the life. These were the first to ridicule and scoff at the true believers after the disappointments. To reveal such hearts—to disclose those who were really glad that Christ had not come—was another of God's purposes in the disappointments.

But the weak, the disloyal, the double-hearted, were not the only ones who were tested. God had led the Millerites just as surely as He had led Israel out of Egypt. And just as He led Israel to the Red Sea that their faith in Him might be tested, so He had led the Millerites through the disappointments that He might test their faith.

But God did not forget or neglect His "little flock" in their time of trial. On the contrary, Jesus looked with sympathy and love upon those who had expected His appearing. Angels hovered around them to sustain them in their disappointment. They were not left in darkness, but again they were led to search their Bibles. Then the concealing hand of the Lord was removed from the mistake, and it was discovered.[11]

We have suggested several reasons for the disappointments, but they may be summarized as follows: First, the two disappointments tested those who really loved Christ's appearing, exposing the false and insincere, and separating them from the true. God was preparing to build His remnant church, and those who were not genuine must be weeded out. Second, each of the disappointments compelled the true believers to turn again to the study of the Scriptures to find additional truth.

---

11 Ellen G. White, *Early Writings*, 236.

So it was that after October 22, 1844, the Adventists were led through the study of the Bible to realize that their disappointment was ordained of God. They saw that the Disappointment was not a mistake, but that it was actually fulfillment of Bible prophecy. They based this conclusion on Revelation 10:9, 10, where John is pictured as "eating" the "little book" which was "sweet as honey" in his mouth, but which became "bitter" when it was swallowed. In no more appropriate way, they felt, could God have symbolized the sweetness of their anticipation of Christ's advent and the bitterness of their disappointment when He failed to appear. Also, in the very next verse they recognized their divine commission to "prophesy again before many peoples, and nations, and tongues, and kings."

A month after the Disappointment, two leading Adventist papers published a lengthy article entitled "Address to the Public." The purpose of the article was twofold: first, to confess frankly that Adventists had been "twice disappointed"; and, second, to show how it was possible to continue to be Adventists in spite of the two disappointments. The article cited Jonah's experience in preaching that "yet forty days and Nineveh shall be overthrown" and pointed out that Nineveh was not overthrown, in spite of Jonah's prophecy. The question was then asked, Was Jonah a false prophet because he preached the *time* of Nineveh's destruction? The answer obviously is No; Jonah had preached what God had told him to preach. The rest was up to God. Jonah's experience, the article stated, serves as a case on record where God caused the preaching of an event at a definite time, although the predicted event did not occur.

The article also referred to Abraham's experience when God commanded him to sacrifice his son Isaac as a test of the faith and obedience of both father and son. In the same way, the article concluded, God had caused the preaching of the Advent message to test the Millerites' faith.

In December, 1844, not long after the second disappointment, God manifested His leadership of the Adventists in a most unusual and remarkable manner. Ellen Harmon, at that time a young woman of 17, was engaged in a season of prayer with four other women in the Haines home in Portland, Maine, when the power of God came upon her. She was given a vision of God's glory and seemed to be rising higher and higher from the earth. Then she was shown some of the experiences of the Adventists as they journeyed to the Holy City.[12]

This proved to be the first of many hundreds of visions and dreams God gave to her during her long life. Through her, during the next seventy years, He guided and counseled His remnant church, verifying many truths that His people discovered through their study of the Bible.

The more we search for an answer to the question Why the disappointment? the more apparent it becomes that God used the Millerite movement to bring into existence His last great reformatory movement. The disappointment of October 22, 1844, was the birth pang of the Seventh-day Adventist Church.

William Miller did not accept all of the new light. He found it impossible to divest himself of the idea that the sanctuary was the earth. Until his death, he was convinced that an error had been made in the date rather than in the event.

In an address given at the Adventist conference held at Low Hampton in December, 1844, Miller stated that he believed a slight discrepancy had been made in the calculations. He stated that there was a difference of "four or five years" in the calculations of the best of the chronologers. On that basis, he argued, it could not honestly be said that they were in error until the time in dispute had passed. Therefore, Miller reasoned, Christ might come at any time. "I have fixed my mind on another time" he wrote a little later, "and here I mean to stand until God gives me more light, and that is, *today, today,* and *today,* until He comes."

An unsympathetic world that was quick to ridicule the Adventists *before* the Disappointment was no less ready to deride them *after* the Disappointment. Much of the fear and solemnity that for a short time restrained the scoffers prior to the Disappointment disappeared with the passing of the time. Many of the tormentors became cruel and brazen in

12 Ibid., 13 ff.

their derision until the Millerites felt as lonely and deserted as did the first disciples at the sepulcher of Christ. Taunting expressions such as "When are you going up?" and "Why have you not gone up yet?" commonly greeted the ears of those who were known to be Adventists. In a letter to a friend, Miller said that on the day after the Disappointment it seemed as though all the demons in the bottomless pit had been turned loose upon the believers. Some, who had been begging for mercy two days before, were now mixing with the rabble, mocking and scoffing in a most blasphemous way.

It is evident that the disappointment of October exposed not two classes of people—the Millerites and the scoffers—but three. The third group was composed of those who had associated with the Millerites and attended their meetings, not because they loved the Lord's appearing, but because they feared it. But the day after the Disappointment these counterfeit Adventists showed their true colors by mocking, scoffing, and threatening those who were sincere.

But the taunting gradually diminished as time passed and as new interests arose to occupy the mind and attention of the world. Thus an era unique in Adventist history came to an end.

CHAPTER 13
1844–1845
TIME OF GLOOM

After the October 22, 1844, disappointment the Millerite movement lost much of its momentum. Energies that might have been used in advancing the cause were dissipated in internal strife and in strengthening individual and "party" interests.

Miller was aware of the divisions. Early in 1845 he wrote that he was "pained at heart" to see the battle in which various factions were engaged. He bemoaned the fact that after having silenced their common enemy, they were turning their weapons against one another. We can touch on only a few of the issues that divided the Millerites.

Most Millerites, including Miller himself, at first felt that the seventh-month movement was of God regardless of the Disappointment. Thousands had been led to study the Scriptures during the "loud cry," and as a result had been reconciled to God. On December 3, Miller wrote that he could see God's hand in the movement.

Others were equally sure that it was Satan who had inspired the seventh-month movement in order to cause confusion. Some Adventists took the position that the specific time contained an error in human calculations, but that the preaching of the Second Coming in connection with the time, so far as it was motivated by a spirit of love for Jesus and mankind, was of God. On the premise that any error would be human rather than divine, they set about to search the Scriptures to learn what the error was.

Most of those who ascribed the seventh-month movement to Satan soon apostatized and left the ranks of the Adventists, some giving up all religious profession in the process. Many of those who attributed the movement entirely to God eventually formed splinter groups that adopted a variety of views and practices, some of which bordered on the fanatical. The result was a widening of the breach between them and another group that recognized God's hand in the movement but was willing to admit its imperfections and to confess the possibility of error.

In order to be consistent, those who credited God with every aspect of the movement were forced to assume that some event related to the fulfillment of prophecy had taken place on October 22. Still clinging to their teaching that Christ was to come on that date, they conceived the idea of an invisible Advent, ignoring the fact that the Bible teaches that "every eye shall see him" (Rev. 1:7). Thus, they said, the door of mercy was already closed; probation was ended, and consequently there was no further need to preach the gospel.

Each of the various splinter groups was eager to gain from Miller some statement that might be interpreted as his endorsement of its views. It was commonly known that Miller took the position that there would be a period just before the actual advent of Christ when He would no longer intercede for the human race, and the Holy Spirit would no longer strive for sinners. It was only natural, then, that those who taught that probation had closed would flood Miller with letters asking his opinion on that point. Miller replied by writing an article that appeared in the *Advent Herald* of February 12, 1845. His reply, however, failed to fulfill the hopes of either the "pros" or the "cons" on the subject.

Miller began by reviewing briefly the history of the seventh-month movement which had culminated in the disappointment of October 22, saying that he could not account for it in any other way than to suppose that God's hand and wisdom were in the movement. He then summarized the types on which the seventh-month idea was based, and went on to say that so far as the close of probation was concerned, it was a delicate subject. If dealt with at all, it should be with much wisdom and humility.

He gave his interpretation of several scriptures, from which he concluded that there would be a period just before the Advent when probation would be closed. But, to the disappointment of many, he did not indicate whether or not he believed that time had arrived. The result was that both of the contending groups claimed his support, which, in the interest of unity, may have been what Miller wanted.

A certain Prof. N. N. Whiting was one of several Millerite ministers who had not accepted the October 22 date. Disappointed in Miller's lack of commitment on the matter of the close of probation, he wrote to him in an attempt to gain a statement that would clarify his views. Miller's reply of March 10, 1845, was quite lengthy and contained an appeal for a period of "at least...two months" during which he hoped discussion on the controversial subject would be discontinued. He expressed the hope that during the period more light would be forthcoming if Christ did not come before its end. In the letter he stated he was not fully convinced probation had closed on October 22.

Because Miller appeared to hesitate in taking a definite stand on some of the points that were at issue among the Adventists after the Disappointment, rumors spread that he had become a puppet in the hands of Himes and other friends; that his opinions were now merely a reflection of the thinking of others. When he became aware of these rumors Miller responded by writing a letter to Himes for publication. In it he acknowledged that he had been accused of allowing the counsel of Himes and others to influence his thinking. But he denied that this was the case, saying that to his knowledge Himes had never attempted to exert an undue influence over him.

Miller had the reputation of being an honest man; even his most bitter opponents never accused him of being otherwise, and there is no reason to doubt the sincerity of his statement. But at this time he was 65 years of age, not old by today's standards, to be sure, but considered old in his day. For a period of thirteen years, from 1831 to 1844, his body and nervous system had been subjected to the almost constant, grueling strain of public platform, and he had experienced more than his share of abuse. He should certainly be forgiven if by 1847 he was beginning to grow a little weary. Since 1839 Himes had been closely associated with Miller in his work.

It would be safe to assume, therefore, that Himes did have some influence on Miller's thinking, perhaps more influence than Miller himself realized. In regard to Miller's being influenced by others, James White wrote after Miller's death that Miller respected and loved his fellow laborers, and any statement that he was not influenced by them to a greater or less extent would be unreasonable.

From the light that God has since given,[1] it is evident that Miller's thinking *was* influenced by others, whom Ellen G. White speaks of as "leading men," without revealing their names. These men used their influence to keep him in darkness and to prevent his accepting the third angel's message after the disappointment of 1844. Had he received this message, he would have understood the reason for the Disappointment. But Miller, whose health was by then broken by hard work in his Master's cause and by age, leaned instead to the human wisdom of his brethren. As a result, he eventually rejected the light of the third angel's message and raised his voice against it. Those who kept him from the truth are more responsible than he for this error; the sin rests upon them.

Although in his letter to N. N. Whiting in March, 1845, Miller wrote that he had not been completely convinced probation closed on October 22, 1844, there was a short period after the Disappointment when he thought his work for the world had finished. He stated this position in the *Advent Herald* of December 11, 1844, in which he said the Adventists had done their work in warning sinners; God in His providence had shut the door, and all they could do was to encourage one another to be patient, to be diligent, and to make their own calling and election sure. But Joshua Himes did not share Miller's view on the "shut door"; he could not bring himself to believe that the work of the church had been completed.

The wide spectrum of views held by various Adventist groups following the Disappointment produced a wide variety of publications to propagate these views. The circulation of so many papers with diverse teachings caused additional confusion and made it difficult for the uninitiated to know the true position of the general body of believers. Miller

[1] Ellen G. White, Early Writings, 257, 258.

relates that during one week he received sixteen different publications, all claiming to be a voice of Adventism; but many of them contained teachings contradictory to the others.

The first person in Miller's local parish who had subscribed fully to his views at the beginning of his public work was a woman with a limited income. Because of her financial situation, Miller made it his practice to pass on to her the papers that came to him, after he was finished with them. One day the woman sent an urgent message, asking him to see her. Supposing that there was an emergency, Miller went to see her.

Upon his arrival she asked, "Have you read these papers?"

"I have looked them over."

"But are they Adventist papers?"

"They profess to be."

"Well, then, I am no longer an Adventist. I shall take the old Bible and stick to that."

"But we have no confidence in half of what is advocated in those papers."

"We? Who is *we*?"

"Why, all of us who stand on the old ground."

"But that ain't telling me who *we* is."

"Well," said Miller in writing the story later, "I was confounded and unable to give her any information on who *we* are."[2]

Other Adventist leaders also recognized the necessity of solidarity. Himes had become the hub of a rather large group who rejected the "shut door" theory. He now became the prime influence in advocating an attempt at unification. In the spring of 1845, Himes, Miller, and Litch united in extending an invitation to all recognized Adventist groups to send delegates to a conference whose purpose was to study existing differences and attempt to minimize them. These meetings, known as the Albany Conference, were the final attempt to weave the remaining strands of the Millerite movement into some definite pattern.

---

2   *A Brief History of William Miller*, 272, 273.

The conference convened for its first session at 9:00 A.M., April 29, 1845, in the Adventist church in Albany, New York. Sixty-one delegates were present, representing nine States and the Province of Ontario. Most of the leaders of the Adventist movement were there, but there were some noteworthy absences. Elder George Storrs, who had introduced to Adventists the Biblical teaching on the sleep of the dead and who had felt himself pushed into accepting a specific date for the Advent, did not attend because of his theological differences. S. S. Snow, who had presented the seventh-month message at the Exeter camp meeting, had in the meantime come under the influence of one Joseph Turner, who for a time was the leader of a radical group. Going beyond Turner's fanaticism, Snow had proclaimed himself to be Elijah the prophet. His extreme ideas had quickly removed him from the mainstream of Adventism. Joseph Bates, who had been speaking at the Exeter camp meeting when Snow's seventh-month idea was first presented there, had learned of the seventh-day Sabbath only a week or two before the Albany Conference. He chose to absent himself from the conference in order to make a trip to Washington, New Hampshire, to learn more about the Sabbath. Charles Fitch, who had become ill as the result of becoming chilled at an outdoor baptism, had died on October 14, 1844, just a few days before the Disappointment. It is obvious that the Adventist movement had experienced more than a little change in leadership in the short time between the Disappointment and the Albany Conference. And with new leadership came new ideas and new philosophies.

There were many questions that divided the Adventists at this time, but there were four that especially demanded the attention of the conference.

One issue was the return of the Jews to Palestine. The idea that the Jews would return to that country either before or after the Second Advent and reestablish a Jewish economy in the land promised to Abraham, had been taught before the rise of Millerism. Miller and his followers had rejected this teaching in the early days of the Millerite movement. But prior to the Albany Conference a small group had accepted the idea and were agitating it among the brethren. Again, at the Albany Conference, this teaching was rejected. The delegates went on record as feeling that "the restoration of the natural Jews, as a nation, either *before* or *after* the second advent of Christ" would be "subversive of the whole gospel system," and stated that they felt bound "to enter our most *solemn protest* against all such teachings."³ With the adoption of this resolution the conference hoped to free itself from the question once and for all, but a small segment, known as the Age to Come Adventists, continued to hold to the teaching.

A second issue that came to the attention of the conference was the newly introduced doctrine that death is an unconscious sleep, and immortality is received only through Christ at His second coming. At the time of the conference most Adventists, including Miller, believed that the dead remain in some state of consciousness, a belief most of them brought with them from their former churches. But some time before the conference Elder George Storrs, a former Methodist minister, had introduced the "new" doctrine. This doctrine was rapidly gaining converts, and was dividing the Adventists into factions in the process. So great an issue had it become that for the conference to have taken a decided stand, pro or con, would have split the group wide open, thus defeating the real purpose of the meetings. The leaders hoped to avoid this happening at all costs; yet the question could not be ignored. Therefore, the conference did not officially express a definite opinion on the condition of man in death. Instead, it evaded the subject by enacting a vague statement "that the departed saints do not enter their inheritance, or receive their crowns, at death."

It seems evident that the conference intentionally avoided addressing itself directly to the question of *what* happens to man at death, and dealt instead with the question of *when* man will receive his reward. Writing later about the experience Miller stated that the question of the intermediate state of the dead did not arise at the conference. The conference, he said, expressed what all Adventists believe, "that the time of the entrance of departed saints into their inheritance is at the resurrection."

3 Ibid., 284.

Four years after her father's death Miller's daughter, then Mrs. Bartholomew, is quoted as saying that if her father had lived one year more, he would undoubtedly have embraced the doctrine that death is an unconscious sleep. Often, just before his death, he would introduce four of his children to his friends as "his four sleepy children" because they believed in the sleep of the dead. But in his *Apology and Defence*, published in 1845, Miller made it clear that he did not consider the doctrine that the dead are unconscious until the resurrection and that the wicked are ultimately destroyed to be true Millerite teachings. This statement was perhaps motivated by the fact that a few Millerite ministers such as George Storrs—and Charles Fitch until he died just before the Disappointment—taught that the dead are unconscious, and Miller wanted to divorce his movement from their teachings.

Writing about Miller at the time of his final illness, Joshua Himes stated that Miller's mind was still clear and strong on the subject of the conscious intermediate state of the dead. James White also indicates that there was no evidence that Miller changed his views on the question of immortality before his death.

Because the question of man's condition in death was not settled completely at the Albany Conference, it plagued Adventists for many years. Eventually most Adventist bodies came to believe in the unconscious state of the dead. But, it seems evident that Miller died believing that man retains some form of consciousness after death.

A third issue dividing the Adventists that required the attention of the conference was the observance of the seventh-day Sabbath. Those who made up the largest segment of the Millerite movement had come from Sunday-keeping churches, and those who came directly into the movement without prior church affiliation observed Sunday in harmony with the almost-universal custom.

But a short time before the Albany Conference Thomas M. Preble, formerly a Freewill Baptist minister, of Washington, New Hampshire, who had become a Millerite preacher, published an article advocating the seventh-day Sabbath.

A reprint fell into the hands of Joseph Bates, who decided to visit Washington to investigate the Sabbath for himself. Although Preble was to discontinue his observance of the seventh-day Sabbath in the middle of 1847, his tract stirred up quite an interest before the Albany Conference convened. It was apparent that the "Seventh-day people" were making serious inroads into the Millerite movement, and the Sabbath question could no longer be ignored.

It is possible that Preble had been influenced by a Seventh-Day Baptist, Mrs. Rachel Oakes (later Preston), who moved to Washington to be near her schoolteacher daughter, Delight Oakes. During her stay in the community she frequently attended the Christian Brethren church in the neighborhood, which, of course, observed Sunday.

One Sunday, when Communion was being observed, the minister, Frederick Wheeler, made the statement that "all who confess communion with Christ in such a service as this should be ready to obey God and keep His commandments in all things." When Mrs. Oakes met Wheeler a few days later while visiting in the home of mutual friends, she reminded him of his statement and told him that she could hardly keep from rising and interrupting the service that Sunday morning. When he asked why, she pointed out that none of the congregation was really keeping all the commandments, since they were completely ignoring the fourth, which enjoins the observance of the seventh day as the Sabbath. This remark struck Wheeler so forcefully that he resolved to study the matter. The result was that he accepted the Sabbath truth and preached his first sermon on that subject in March, 1844.

Perhaps no other incident in Millerite history better illustrates the interdenominational character of the Millerite movement than this discovery of "new light" on the Sabbath in Washington, New Hampshire. Here was Rachel Oakes, a Seventh-Day Baptist, sharing her faith with Wheeler, a Methodist minister turned Millerite, who was preaching in a Christian Brethren church.

William Miller was a Baptist. Ellen White was a Methodist. James White was a member of the Christian Connection.

Joseph Bates belonged to the Christian Church. Joshua V. Himes, when he became associated with William Miller, was preaching for the Massachusetts Christian Conference. Josiah Litch was a Methodist. Charles Fitch was a Congregational minister, later turned Presbyterian. And so the list could go on.

In the spring of 1844 Litch stated that those who were preaching for the Millerites were known to have come from at least thirteen different religious bodies.

We must conclude that of all religious movements the Millerite movement was one of the most ecumenical in nature. It was illustrative of the truth that God always has sincere seekers after truth in every religious body.

To return to Washington, New Hampshire. Soon after Frederick Wheeler accepted the Sabbath truth several other members of the little church followed him, thus becoming, in a limited sense, the first group of Seventh-day Adventist laymen. And Rachel Oakes accepted the Advent truth, and thus she also became a Seventh-day Adventist, since she was already a Sabbathkeeper as a Seventh-Day Baptist.

Those who accepted the Sabbath truth were automatically dropped from the Christian Brethren Church, so they conducted their meetings in private homes for some time. Eventually their number in the community increased. Shortly after the group organized as a church, in 1862, it acquired the Christian Brethren church property. The little church had been built in the early 1840's in what was then a prosperous community. Since then, a diminishing population has left it somewhat isolated. But the church still stands in the shaded woods near Millen Pond on the outskirts of the village of Washington, New Hampshire.

As might be expected, the 1845 Albany Conference was not sympathetic with the Sabbath question. It went on record as being "*Resolved*, that we can have no sympathy or fellowship with those things which have only a shadow of wisdom in will-worship and neglecting of the body, after the commandments and doctrines of men. That we have no fellowship with any of the *new tests* as conditions of salvation....That we have no fellowship for Jewish fables and commandments of men, that turn from the truth, or for any of the distinctive characteristics of modern Judaism."[4] It is to be noted that the committee that drew up the resolution, of which Miller was chairman, avoided the term *Sabbath*, referring to its observance rather as "Jewish fables and commandments of men." The committee had no way of knowing that in a few years the "Seventh-day party," unified not only by its belief in the Sabbath but also by its acceptance of the manifestations of the Spirit of Prophecy in the person of Ellen G. White, would become the largest of the several Adventist groups to trace its ancestry back to the Millerite movement.

So far as Miller is concerned, he retained his original view on the matter of the Sabbath, as well as of the state of the dead. To the last, as far as can be determined, he considered the seventh-day Sabbath as "Jewish fables and commandments of men." It may seem strange to us today that the man whose mind could fathom the intricacies of the 2300-day prophecy could not see the simple and beautiful truths of man's condition in death and of the seventh-day Sabbath.

But such a situation is by no means unusual. More than a few times in the history of the church men who have been used of God to reveal certain truths to His people have themselves sometimes been unable to see additional light that has come to them. The reasons for this are perhaps to be found in the peculiar character of the human mind. Sometimes, in the inscrutable ways of God, it may be His plan that they do not see. And, as we previously pointed out, it is possible that Miller was influenced in his thinking during his closing years by some of his associates.

Of the several issues dividing the Adventist body that came to the attention of the Albany Conference, none was more threatening to the movement's unity than the "shut door" theory, which theory we discussed briefly in a previous chapter. This teaching held that if Christ had fulfilled the prophecy of Daniel 8:14 by entering the Most Holy Place of the heavenly sanctuary to carry on His work as high priest on October 22, as many Adventists believed, He must thereby have shut the door on His meditorial work in the

4   Ibid., 285, 286.

first room or the holy place. Therefore the door of salvation was forever closed; no longer could sinners be saved. Miller at first accepted the shut door teaching, as did Joseph Bates, James White, and nearly all other Adventists, including Ellen Harmon. Himes, who believed that because Christ had not come the door was not shut, and who therefore differed with Miller on the question, became the leader of an increasingly large group who shared his views. Others, such as Josiah Litch and Joseph Marsh, had at one time advocated the theory but had repudiated it and sided with Himes before the Albany Conference was called. There were still others, such as Sylvester Bliss, Elon Galusha, and George Storrs, who from the first had refused to accept the idea of a "shut door," and they too joined with Himes. It was to a large degree Himes's hope of obtaining harmony on this point that caused him to join Miller in calling the Albany Conference. In the meantime, under Himes's influence, Miller began to waver on the point. Eventually he lined up with Himes and his group.

Under these circumstances it is not surprising that the Albany Conference rejected the "shut door" idea and placed itself on record, "that it is the duty of the ministers of the word to continue in the work of preaching the gospel to every creature, even unto the end, calling upon them to repent, in view of the fact that the kingdom of heaven is at hand."

With the passing of time, the question of the "shut door" became less important in the thinking of the Adventists. Its advocates had difficulty supporting the idea from the Bible; the fact that people continued to be converted, contradicted it; and children who had been too young to be accountable in 1844, were reaching the age of decision. Surely they were not to be denied salvation merely because they had been born "too late."

There were those who feared that the Albany Conference would be marked by internal strife and open discord, that it would only serve to emphasize the existing differences. But this did not prove to be the case. In general, harmony prevailed. Miller and Himes provided strong leadership and structured the meetings so as to minimize the possibility of open discord, and, as has already been noted, several of the potentially discordant persons absented themselves from the meetings.

The conference, however, fell far short of its goal of restoring unity to the ranks of Adventists. It succeeded in strengthening the feeling of unity within certain "parties," or groups, of Adventists, but it failed to bind these groups together. The differences were now too great, and there was too little in common.

The one unifying element was a belief in the advent of Christ. But even in this there were now divergent views. In other areas there was a host of different teachings that led eventually to the establishment of four religious bodies, all of which traced their ancestry to the Millerite movement. These were the Advent Christians, Evangelical Adventists, The Life and Advent Union, and the Seventh-day Adventists.

Not all Adventists were happy with the Albany Conference. Some questioned the wisdom of drawing up anything even resembling a statement of belief, fearing that this would lead to the formation of a creed, and that Adventists would become another formal church, part of "Babylon." Presumably, the dissatisfaction that was expressed came from those who had not attended the conference, for Miller states that had there been a dissenting voice on the passage of any act, it would have been promptly reconsidered. Regardless of how democratic the conference was, it was so misunderstood, criticized, and opposed that Miller felt it necessary, or at least prudent, to come to its defense. This defense was written May 27, 1845, almost exactly one month from the convening of the conference. It is probable that Miller's lengthy explanation succeeded in pacifying the critics to some extent, for the actions of the conference were unanimously ratified at two conferences later that year, in New York City and in Boston.

Although Miller and Himes continued to travel, preach, and publish, the Millerite cause as such exerted very little influence after the Albany Conference. The movement that earlier had been characterized by unity, enthusiasm, and love, was after the Albany Conference divided, torn by dissension and jealousy, and almost completely spent of its power. Its time of glory was past, and days of gloom had come.

CHAPTER 14
1845–1849
THE SILENCED VOICE

Most of the members of the small Baptist church in Miller's hometown of Low Hampton espoused his cause, or at least were sympathetic with it. But there was a small vociferous and influential minority who opposed him and his followers. As a result of the agitation of this group, a council composed of seven ministers and ten laymen was called to meet on January 29, 1845, to study Miller's case. This action had the natural effect of widening the already existing breach in the church, solidifying the position of both sides, and placing the Millerite-favoring majority more solidly against the minority.

The anti-Millerites submitted to the council a list of charges against Miller and his sympathizers. This list was prefaced by the explanation that the church felt that the Millerites had departed from the beliefs of the Baptist denomination; that they had accepted and taught doctrines that time had proved false; and that, in so doing, they had caused dissension and discord in the church. This statement was followed by a list of seven accusations against Miller or the Millerites.

The first accusation was aimed directly at Miller. It stated that "we are grieved that the brethren claiming to be the church should have employed, in the year 1843, contrary to our expressed wishes, a man of avowed sentiments that the second advent of Christ would take place in the year 1843, and whose known purpose was to preach the doctrine."[1]

In returning its verdict, the council upheld all the charges against the Millerites except one—that they had appropriated church property for their own use. The council made it plain that the minority—that is, the non-Millerites—was to be considered "the regular Baptist church in Hampton," and

---

1   *A Brief History of William Miller*, 258.

that the Millerites could be reinstated as members "upon suitable confession."

The rendering and accepting of this report early in 1845 brought to an end Miller's association with the Baptist Church, which had covered a period of about thirty years.

When this action was taken Miller was 63 years old, and could feel the infirmities of old age beginning to take their toll. As the guiding spirit of a movement that had resulted in disappointment to thousands of sincere Christians, he felt obligated to make a last statement about his work and motives. With this purpose in mind, he wrote his *Apology and Defence* in July, 1845. This appeared as a thirty-six-page pamphlet published by Joshua V. Himes, and was addressed "To all who love the Lord Jesus Christ in sincerity."

He began by stating that he felt the public was entitled to a statement from him in regard to the Disappointment, since all men have a responsibility to their community for the ideas they promulgate. In fulfilling his responsibility Miller endeavored to place before the public a retrospective view of the entire Millerite movement and the motives that prompted it. There followed a review of his labors and their results in turning men's minds and hearts toward God. In view of the good that had been accomplished, he was convinced that his work had been to God's glory in spite of what he considered to have been error in computing the time. This pamphlet was the last important work to come from his pen.

Miller did very little public work the rest of the year. On the eleventh of December he wrote, "I am much troubled with my old complaint. Bless the Lord, I hope to be with him soon." Three months later he went with Himes and Apollos Hale to Glen's Falls, New York, where he gave a series of lectures. On June 24, he arrived in Cranberry Creek, New York, where he gave seven lectures in four days. He did very little writing during the remaining summer months.

His next article appeared in the *Advent Herald,* September 9, 1846. In it Miller stated he was thankful that he had never pretended to be divinely inspired, but had always directed his hearers to the same source that he used; that is, the Bible. At no time did he claim to be anything other than one who had studied the Bible carefully and prayerfully, who had arrived at certain well-thought-out conclusions, and who had a conviction that God wanted him to make these conclusions known to as many people as possible. He laid no claim to being a "prophet"; it was the Bible, not William Miller, that was inspired.

His statement about not being divinely inspired could be interpreted as an oblique reference to Ellen Harmon, who had been given her first vision in December of 1844, but which had not been published until 1846, the same year Miller wrote the statement referred to above. He seems not to have accepted the work of Ellen G. White as the manifestation of the Spirit of Prophecy. However, to impute to Miller's statement any allusion to Ellen Harmon's visions is to add words that are not there. Such an interpretation is not in keeping with his character. It is most likely that he intended the sentence to be a simple statement of fact. There is nothing in the context to indicate otherwise. The timing was probably coincidental.

It was about this time that Miller offered some practical advice to those who might be inclined to be critical of those whose religious convictions differed from their own. It was typical of Miller that his advice should contain a touch of humor.

When you are tempted to write to a brother to complain about his opinions, Miller advised, it would be well to wait three days before you do so. During that time, pray nine times that God will direct in what you write. Then, if you write the letter, go to the brother's house and read the letter to yourself three times. Seal it only if you can honestly say that you love the brother, and mail it only if you would like to be the one who delivers it. And while the letter is in the mail, think of the tears of joy the brother will shed when he receives it. "And," Miller added, "remember to pay postage."

On September 22 Miller gave two lectures in South Troy, Vermont. During the evening lecture the building was pelted with eggs and stones. One stone, about the size of an egg, crashed through a window and struck the desk at which Miller was speaking. He paused and then asked, "Is this Vermont, the State that boasts of its freedom, of its republicanism? Shame on Vermont!" The meeting then proceeded without additional interruption.

Early in 1848 Miller began to lose his sight, which deteriorated rapidly, so that he could not read. The difficulty, according to the doctor, was with the retinas. It became necessary for him to dictate his letters.

In March his son, Robbins, took the lens from a "spyglass," or telescope, and held it before his father's eye. With it Miller could read a few words. He was able to distinguish one object from another, and could usually recognize friends and acquaintances. But even with the strongest glasses then available, he could read very little.

Occasionally he attempted to write, although he could hardly see the letters he formed. The entire procedure was frustrating, and the result was far from satisfactory. One such attempt was a letter written in the spring of 1849, in large letters and obviously with a shaky hand. The letter was never completed, and the salutation, "Dear Brother," gives no clue as to its intended reader. Perhaps it was Himes. It begins, "I cannot refrain from writing a word or two, although I cannot see. All is well."

Beginning the last of April, 1849, Miller's general health began to fail. The annual conference of Adventists, in session in New York, passed a resolution conveying to him their sympathy, assuring him of their prayers, and expressing their hope of meeting him in the new earth. Miller was deeply touched when the message was read to him. In his dictated reply, he expressed doubt at his ever seeing them again in this life, reaffirmed his confidence in the Saviour's advent, and exhorted his friends to remain faithful.

He suffered much during the summer and fall months, and his strength and sight continued to fail, although his mind remained clear and sharp. During the autumn and winter of 1849 he was confined almost entirely to his room, and spent most of his time in bed. On the thirteenth of December he experienced a very severe attack of pain. His family, fearing he would not live through the night, sent for Himes. But, for some reason, Himes did not arrive at the Miller home until the morning of the seventeenth. By that time Miller's condition had improved so that he recognized Himes's voice when he entered the room and spoke Miller's name.

However, on the morning of December 20 it became apparent that the end was near. Miller sank into a peaceful sleep, although he occasionally roused and opened his eyes for brief periods. But he could not speak. His breathing gradually became shorter and shorter until it ceased entirely at five minutes after three in the afternoon. He was 67 years and 10 months of age. Thus was silenced the urgent voice of the grand old man of the Second Advent movement.

At his bedside, in addition to members of the family, was Joshua Himes. How appropriate it was that the one who ten years before had committed himself to the task of promoting Miller's views "to the ends of the earth" should be present to bid him a last farewell.

Miller had requested to be buried from the Adventist chapel at Low Hampton, but the family felt that the building was too small to accommodate all who would wish to attend the services, so other plans were made.

At 10:00 A.M., Sunday, December 23, the family and close friends gathered in the Miller home, where a brief private service was conducted. Joshua Himes read portions of Scripture, a hymn was sung by the Fairhaven church choir, and prayer was offered.

Following this private service, Miller was laid to rest in the cemetery about half a mile from the Miller home. Himes recorded that about one hundred sleighs followed in the procession. Immediately after the burial a public memorial service was held in the Congregational church, which was much larger than the Adventist chapel.

Near the top of the marker on Miller's grave is the inscription, "At the time appointed the end shall be" (Dan. 8:19); and near the base of the marker is inscribed the verse "But go thy way till the end be, for thou shalt rest, and stand in thy lot at the end of the days."

We can best appreciate the appropriateness of these inscriptions when we view them in the light of the following statement from God's messenger:

"God suffered him [Miller] to fall under the power of Satan, the dominion of death, and hid him in the grave from those who were constantly drawing him from the truth. Moses erred as he was about to enter the Promised Land. So also, I saw that William Miller erred as he was soon to enter the heavenly Canaan, in suffering his influence to go against the truth. Others led him to this; others must account for it. But *angels watch the precious dust of this servant of God, and he will come forth at the sound of the last trump.*"[2] (Italics supplied.)

In narrating the story of William Miller, we have repeatedly used the term "Millerite movement" because it is a common name, and a very convenient one. But in a way it is a misleading term. The movement was really not of Miller, it was of God. Miller was only the instrument whom God used to nurture the spiritual soil so that out of it might spring His remnant church.

Perhaps, then, there is no better way to conclude this account of Miller's life and work than to review a significant paragraph written by another whom God chose to guide His people in these last days:

"In reviewing our past history, having traveled over every step of advance to our present standing, I can say, Praise God! As I see what the Lord has wrought, I am filled with astonishment, and with confidence in Christ as leader. *We have nothing to fear for the future, except as we shall forget the way the Lord has led us, and His teaching in our past history.*"[3] (Italics supplied.)

---

2   Ellen G. White, *Early Writings*, 258.
3   Ellen G. White, *Life Sketches* (Mountain View, California: Pacific Press, 1943), 196.

APPENDIX

IMPORTANT DATES AND EVENTS IN WILLIAM MILLER'S LIFE

1782, February 15. Born at Pittsfield, Massachusetts.
1786. Family moved to Low Hampton, New York.
1803, June 29. Married Lucy Smith of Poultney, Vermont.
1810. Entered military service.
1815. Retired from military service; moved family from Poultney, Vermont, back to Low Hampton, New York, where he made his home the rest of his life.
1816. Became a Christian and joined the Baptist church at Low Hampton, New York. Began a thorough study of Bible prophecy, especially Daniel 8:14.
1831, Summer. Gave his first study on the Second Advent, at Dresden, New York.
1833, September. Received a license to preach, issued by the Baptist church at Low Hampton, New York.
1833, November 13. "Falling of the stars" gave impetus to Millerite movement.
1835, March. Received a second certificate to preach, from Baptist Church.
1839, November. Joshua V. Himes became associated with Miller.
1840, February 28. First issue of the *Signs of the Times*.
1840, March 11–23. First series of lectures in Casco Street church, Portland, Maine, attended by Ellen Harmon.
1842, May 24. General conference session held at Boston; Joseph Bates presiding. Fitch and Hale introduced their "chart." Plan made for conducting Millerite camp meetings.
1842, June 4–12. Second series of lectures held in Portland, Maine.
1842, June 28. Camp meeting at East Kingston. "Great Tent" offering taken.

1844, March 21. First disappointment.

1844, August 12–17. Exeter camp meeting. Seventh-month idea presented by Samuel S. Snow. Beginning of the "Loud Cry."

1844, October 22. Second disappointment. Beginning of investigative judgment.

1845, January 29. Miller and followers dropped from Baptist church at Low Hampton.

1845, April 29. Albany Conference convened. Final attempt to unify the Millerite movement.

1845, July. Miller wrote *Apology and Defence*.

1849, December 20, 3:05 P.M. Miller's death.

1849, December 23. Memorial services and burial near Miller home in Low Hampton.

TEACH Services, Inc.
P U B L I S H I N G

We invite you to view the complete
selection of titles we publish at:
www.TEACHServices.com

We encourage you to write us
with your thoughts about this,
or any other book we publish at:
info@TEACHServices.com

TEACH Services' titles may be purchased in
bulk quantities for educational, fund-raising,
business, or promotional use.
bulksales@TEACHServices.com

Finally, if you are interested in seeing
your own book in print, please contact us at:
publishing@TEACHServices.com

We are happy to review your manuscript at no charge.

www.ingramcontent.com/pod-product-compliance
Lightning Source LLC
Chambersburg PA
CBHW070555160426
43199CB00014B/2508